Trending Topics

College English through a Cultural Lens

Myeong-Hee Seong, Daniel Cuffey

지식인

Authors

Myeong-Hee Seong

Ph.D. in English Education, Korea University
Professor, Eulji University

Daniel Cuffey

M.Ed. International Education, University of Illinois
Professor, Eulji University

Trending Topics

College English through a Cultural Lens

2021년 8월 5일 초판 1쇄 인쇄
2021년 8월 10일 초판 1쇄 발행

지은이 | Myeong-Hee Seong · Daniel Cuffey
펴낸이 | 김종욱 · 명사동
펴낸곳 | 지식인
등 록 | 제301-2013-134호
주 소 | 서울시 도봉구 도봉로 180길 20 투웨니퍼스트 102동 602호
전 화 | 02)2266-8606
팩 스 | 02)2266-8607
E-mail | jisikin2013@naver.com
홈페이지 | www.jisikinbook.co.kr

ISBN 979-11-90815-75-8 (93740)

값 16,000원

Trending Topics

College English through a Cultural Lens

A Note from the Authors

This book is designed to spark interesting discussions in university English classes while helping students develop their speaking, reading, writing, and listening skills.
Every unit focuses on a cultural difference or social issue, along with related songs. The songs have been added to give students a deeper understanding of the topics and to provide some lively listening practice.
The songs and movies selected are primarily from the United States, but we encourage learners to compare what is in this textbook with entertainment from other cultures for a more diverse experience.

Good luck on your path to English mastery!

Table of Contents

Chapter 1: Cultural Differences

Chapter 2: Social Issues

Trending Topics

Trending Topics

CHAPTER 1

Cultural Differences

Trending
Topics

UNIT 1
Communication

TOPICS

- Gender Differences
- Nonverbal Communication

ICEBREAKERS

- How would you describe your communication style?
- Do you think men or women use more nonverbal communication?

Vocabulary Preview

A. *Matching*

1. stimulus (n.) ______	a. make something appear larger than it is
2. extensive (adj.) ______	b. set apart from the rest or from each other
3. magnify (v.) ______	c. similarity between different things
4. segregate (v.) ______	d. a thing that rouses activity or energy in someone
5. negotiate (v.) ______	e. not involving or using words or speech
6. symmetry (n.) ______	f. essential or fundamental
7. nonverbal (adj.) ______	g. large in amount or scale
8. integral (adj.) ______	h. obtain or bring about by discussion

B. *Fill in the blanks using the vocabulary words above.*

1. Some schools ________________ students according to their academic abilities.
2. The customer tried to ________________ a lower price.
3. The dog responded to the ________________ of the ringing bell.
4. Math is an ________________ part of the school's curriculum.
5. A microscope is needed to ________________ the tiny insect.
6. He expected the woman to understand his ________________ cues.
7. She has ________________ experience in her field. She has been working there for 30 years.
8. This extra room may interfere with the ________________ of the building.

Language Focus (Nouns)

Choose the best option to complete the following sentences.

1. For men, communication is a way to negotiate for power, seek wins, avoid failure and offer _______, among other things.
   a. an advice b. advice
   c. advices d. advise

2. _______ of this communication takes place using nonverbal cues.
   a. Much b. Many
   c. Every d. Any

3. His diaries contain _______ about the alleged bribery.
   a. informations b. the informations
   c. an information d. information

4. ABC Outlet is the leading _______ of air conditioners in this area.
   a. distributors b. distributing
   c. distribution d. distributor

5. I wonder when _______ will be noticeable on the construction project.
   a. progresses b. progressions
   c. progress d. progressed

6. Dress well and give a firm handshake when applying for a job, because first _______ are very important.
   a. impress b. impressed
   c. impressions d. impressionable

7. According to the recipe, you need _______ in order to make the cake.
   a. some flours b. many flours
   c. many flour d. some flour

Communication Styles

It is commonly said that men and women are so different, they must be from other planets. This expression was popularized by John Gray's famous book *Men Are from Mars, Women Are from Venus*. This book highlights the fact that men and women clearly have diverse ways of thinking and communicating. Just think of how you would respond to a particular stimulus and how someone of the opposite sex might respond if faced with the same situation. Through extensive research, clear differences have been found between the two genders.

Rather than looking into why there's a difference, we often magnify stereotypes or focus on the surface-level issues. Growing up, boys and girls are often segregated, restricting them to socialize solely with individuals of their own gender, learning a distinct culture as well as their gender's norms. This results in the communicative differences so commonly seen between men and women.

For example, men are more likely to communicate as a way to maintain their status and independence, while women tend to view communication as a path to create friendships and build relationships. For men, communication is a way to negotiate for power, seek wins, avoid failure and offer advice. For women, communication is a way to get closer, seek understanding and find equality or symmetry.

A lot of this communication takes place using nonverbal cues. According to *Psychology Today*, more than half of all communication is nonverbal. Nonverbal communication is integral to how we communicate but males and females use different nonverbal cues. Men generally use fewer facial expressions than women. Men also smile less. Women tend to rely heavily on facial expressions, including head nodding and eye contact. This is because, as children, they were taught more appeasement body language according to *Science of People*.

Communication styles also differ between high-context and low-context cultures. High-context cultures rely heavily on nonverbal communication to convey meaning. In contrast, low-context cultures depend largely on words themselves. Communication tends to be more direct and hierarchies are more relaxed. Eastern cultures are generally considered high-context while Western cultures are typically low-context.

As you can see, communication styles vary widely based on gender and culture.

Reading Comprehension

Circle the correct words to complete the sentences.

1. Growing up, boys and girls are often (segregation / segregated).
2. Men are more likely (to communicate / communicating) as a way to maintain their status.
3. Communication is a way (negotiating / to negotiate) for power and offer advice.
4. A lot of communication takes place using (nonverbally / nonverbal) cues.
5. Men use (less / fewer) facial expressions than women.

Questions

1. How do men and women communicate differently?

2. Do you think nonverbal communication is important? Why?

Free Writing

Do you think men are from Mars and women are from Venus? Write a short paragraph explaining your opinion.

____

____

____

____

____

____

____

____

____

Cultural Spotlight: *Hollywood's Portrayal of Women*

Hollywood movies have often magnified and reinforced gender stereotypes throughout history. The film industry has only recently started to face criticism for this common tendency, but researchers in academia have taken note for a long time. A famous study by Bussey and Bandura in *Psychological Review* in 1999 noted that "women are portrayed as dependent on other characters, over-emotional, and confined to low-status jobs when compared to enterprising and ambitious male characters."

Many believe that this stereotypical representation of women is changing or has already changed in Hollywood, but recent studies have shown otherwise. A study by Dr. Martha Lauzen in 2015 found that "women comprised less than a third of speaking parts in the top grossing domestic films in 2013." Women also only accounted for "15% of the protagonists" in the same study. Lauzen went on to say "The truth is, even in the latest films, female characters are two times more likely than males to be identified only by a life-related role rather than a work-related role." This means women are still identified as mothers, daughters, or lovers instead of bankers, police officers, or action heroes. Lauzen also notes that women are "rarely portrayed as formal leaders."

One classic Hollywood movie that provides an interesting study on the differences between male and female communication is *The Way We Were*. This movie was released in 1973 and is considered one of the greatest love stories of all time. Some people believe that this movie broke the typical Hollywood mold by portraying a strong female character.

The Way We Were is the story of Katie Morosky and Hubbell Gardiner. Their differences are immense. She is a stridently vocal Marxist with strong anti-war opinions and he is carefree with no particular political bent. While attending the same college, she is drawn to him because of his boyish good looks and his natural writing skill, although he does not work very hard at it. He is intrigued by her conviction and her determination to persuade others to take up social causes. Their attraction is evident, but neither of them acts upon it, and they lose touch after graduation.

The two meet again towards the end of World War II, while Katie is working at a radio station and Hubbell is trying to return to civilian life after serving as a naval officer. They fall in love despite the differences in their backgrounds and temperaments. Hubbell is then offered the opportunity to adapt a novel he wrote into a screenplay, but Katie believes he is wasting his talent and encourages him to pursue writing as a serious challenge instead. Despite her growing frustration, they move to California where, without much effort, he becomes a successful screenwriter and they enjoy an affluent lifestyle. As the Hollywood blacklist grows and McCarthyism begins to encroach on their lives, Katie's political activism resurfaces, jeopardizing Hubbell's position and reputation.

Alienated by Katie's persistent abrasiveness, and though she is pregnant, Hubbell has a liaison with his college girlfriend and the divorcee of his best friend. Katie and Hubbell decide to part after the birth of their child, as Katie finally understands he is not the man she idealized when falling in love with him. She thinks he will always choose the easiest way out, whether it is cheating in his marriage or writing predictable stories for sitcoms. Hubbell feels exhausted and unable to live up to the goals Katie created for him.

Katie and Hubbell meet by chance some years after their divorce. Hubbell is with a stylishly beautiful woman and, apparently content, is now writing for a television show. Katie, now remarried, invites Hubbell to come for a drink with his lady, but he turns down the invitation. Hubbell inquires about their daughter

Rachel, and if Katie's new husband is a good father to her. He shows no intention of meeting her, implying that he has not been a part of Rachel's life in the past, nor does he plan to be in her life in the future, to which Katie seems resigned, but content.

Katie has remained faithful to who she is; flyers in hand, she is agitating now for "Ban the bomb," the new political cause. Their past is behind them, and all the two share now (besides their daughter) is missing what they once had together, the memory of the way things were.

Sentence Structure: ***Make sentences using the examples below.***

1. by chance

   ex) Katie and Hubbell meet by chance some years after their divorce.

   ____

2. turn down

   ex) He turns down the invitation.

   ____

3. break the mold

   ex) Some people believe that this movie broke the typical Hollywood mold.

   ____

Cultural Spotlight: Music

Listen and circle the correct words. (1)

The Way We Were (Barbra Streisand)

Memories
(Light / Right) the corners of my mind
Misty watercolor memories
Of the way we were

Scattered pictures
(Of / Off) the smiles we left behind
Smiles we gave to one another
For the way we were

Can it be that it was all so simple then?
Or has time rewritten every line?
If we (have / had) the chance to do it all again
Tell me, would we?
Could we?

Memories
May be beautiful and yet
What's (to / too) painful to remember
We simply choose to forget

So it's the laughter
We will remember
(Whenever / Wherever) we remember
The way we were
The way we were

Listen and circle the correct words. (2)

Speechless (Naomi Scott)

Here comes a wave (mean / meant)
to wash me away
A tide that is taking me under
Swallowing sand
Left with nothing to say
My voice (drown / drowned) out in
the thunder
But I (want / won't) cry
And I won't start to crumble
Whenever they try to shut me or cut
me down
I won't be (silence / silenced)
You can't keep me quiet
Won't tremble when you try it
All I know is I won't go speechless
'Cause I'll (breath / breathe)
When they try to suffocate me
Don't you underestimate me
'Cause I know that I won't go
speechless
Written in stone
Every rule, every word
Centuries old and unbending
Stay in your place
Better seen and not heard
But now that story is ending
'Cause I
I cannot start to crumble
So come on and try
Try to shut me and cut me down
I won't be silenced
You can't keep me quiet
Won't tremble when you try it
All I know is I won't go speechless,
speechless
Let the storm in
I cannot be broken
No, I won't (live / leave) unspoken
'Cause I know that I won't go
speechless
Try to lock me in this cage
I won't just lay me down and (die /
dye)
I will take these broken wings
And watch me burn across the sky
Hear the echo saying
I won't be (silence / silenced)
Though you wanna see me tremble
when you try it
All I know is I won't go speechless,
speechless,
'Cause I'll (breath / breathe)
When they try to suffocate me
Don't you underestimate me
'Cause I know that I won't go
speechless
All I know is I won't go speechless

Listen and fill in the blanks. (1)

The Way We Were (Barbra Streisand)

Memories
Light the ( )
Misty watercolor memories
Of the way we were

( ) pictures
Of the smiles we left behind
Smiles we gave to one another
For the way we were

Can it be that it was all so simple then?
Or has time rewritten every line?
If we ( ) to do it all again
Tell me, would we?
Could we?

Memories
May be beautiful and yet
What's too painful to remember
We simply choose to forget

So it's the laughter
We will remember
( )
The way we were
The way we were

Listen and fill in the blanks. (2)

Speechless (Naomi Scott)

Here comes a (   ) wash me away
A tide that is taking me under
Swallowing sand
Left with nothing to say
My voice (   ) in the thunder
But I (   )
And I won't start to crumble
Whenever they try to shut me or cut me down
I (   )
You can't keep me quiet
Won't tremble when you try it
All I know is I won't go speechless
'Cause (   )
When they try to suffocate me
Don't you underestimate me
'Cause I know that I won't go speechless
Written in stone
Every rule, every word
Centuries old and unbending
Stay in your place
Better seen and not heard
But now that story is ending
'Cause I
I cannot start to crumble
So come on and try
Try to shut me and cut me down
I (   )
You can't keep me quiet
Won't tremble when you try it
All I know is I won't go speechless, speechless
Let the storm in
I cannot be broken
No, I won't live unspoken
'Cause I know that I won't go speechless
Try to (   ) in this cage
I won't just lay me down and die
I will take these broken wings
And watch me (   )the sky
Hear the (   ) saying
I won't be silenced
Though you wanna see me tremble when you try it
All I know is I won't go speechless, speechless,
'Cause (   )
When they try to suffocate me
Don't you underestimate me
'Cause I know that I won't go speechless
All I know is I won't go speechless

Wrap-Up

Share your opinions:

1. Do you think it's difficult to communicate with men?
2. Do you think it's difficult to communicate with women?
3. Do you use a lot of nonverbal communication?
4. Do you live in a high-context or low-context culture?
5. Can you think of any popular movies with a strong female lead?

Hollywood Movies

Pros	Cons

UNIT 2
Youth

TOPICS
- Adolescence
- Coming-of-Age Stories

ICEBREAKERS
- What were your hobbies when you were young?
- Would you rather live alone or with your parents?

Vocabulary Preview

A. *Matching*

1. adulthood (n.) ______
2. vigor (n.) ______
3. adolescent (adj.) ______
4. differentiate (v.) ______
5. mindset (n.) ______
6. ambiguous (adj.) ______
7. guardian (n.) ______
8. construct (v.) ______

a. physical strength and good health
b. recognize what makes something different
c. the established set of attitudes held by someone
d. in the process of developing from a child into an adult
e. the state or condition of being fully grown
f. unclear or inexact
g. build something; form an idea
h. defender, protector, or parent

B. *Fill in the blanks using the vocabulary words above.*

1. This car is more expensive but I can't see any features that ________________ it from last year's model.
2. Her ________________ mind thinks her mother should give her more freedom.
3. The ending of the story was ________________. The reader is left with a lot of questions.
4. You need to exercise regularly if you want to retain your youthful ________________.
5. His aunt is his legal ________________.
6. They plan to ________________ a new garage for their cars.
7. His childhood problems persisted into ________________.
8. You need to work hard and keep a positive ________________.

Language Focus (Pronouns)

Choose the best option to complete the following sentences.

1. It could hurt, not only ______, but also her children.

   a. she b. hers
   c. herself d. her

2. The NPAD leader made a speech on Thursday, a day after Mr. Lee made ______.

   a. him b. himself
   c. his d. his's

3. Ms. Park had allowed ______ to be distracted.

   a. her b. hers
   c. she d. herself

4. Some expected him to come back soon, ______ disagreed with it.

   a. the other b. others
   c. another d. anothers

5. Northern European countries have a better social welfare system than ______ of the USA.

   a. those b. that
   c. these d. this

6. It's all up to ______. Let's hope that he has what it takes.

   a. he b. his own
   c. him d. he's

7. Our storage facilities are inexpensive when compared to ______ of Super Storage down the street.

   a. it b. those
   c. them d. that

Youth Development

The terms *youth*, *adolescent*, *teenager*, and *young person* often mean the same thing, but they are occasionally differentiated. These terms can be ambiguous when applied to someone of an older age, potentially when still dependent on their guardians. The United Nations defines *youth* as people between the ages of 15 and 24. Regardless of the specific age range we use, it is clear that young people around the world share a similar mindset despite growing up in very different environments.

Universally, youth are in the process of constructing the self-concept. Generally, the *self-concept* embodies the answer to "Who am I?" This represents a collection of beliefs about yourself and is influenced by variables such as your peers, lifestyle, gender, and culture. This is a time when young people discover their true identities and their choices are most likely to affect their future. It is also the stage of life when one is energetic, full of vigor and maturing before adulthood

Your particular experience shapes the extent to which you still rely on your family emotionally and economically. This is called your *level of dependency* and it varies according to different cultural perspectives. In some parts of the world it is common to live with your parents until you are married, while in other cultures young people move away from home much earlier.

Additionally, young people in many developing countries are forced to work at an early age in order to help support their families. This would be unthinkable in many developed countries. The United Nations predicts that the youth population in the poorest countries around the world will be 62% higher by 2050. This means that a growing population of young people around the world will have different values and dependency levels when compared to young people in wealthier countries.

Research has shown that cultural values are relatively enduring and have an effect on youth development. Perhaps the most well-known of these broad cultural values are individualism and collectivism. Individualists are largely driven by pursuits that benefit themselves, while collectivists place a high value on the well-being of the larger group, typically their family, workplace, or country. Growing up within a family or culture that promotes individualism or collectivism can alter the way a young person behaves and views the world.

As you can see, the universal experience of growing up differs in an endless number of ways depending on your particular situation.

Reading Comprehension

Circle the correct words to complete the sentences.

1. Youth is an (experiencing / experience) that may shape an individual's level of dependency.
2. Youth can be referred to as the (time of life / lifetime) when one is young.
3. The United Nations (defining / defines) youth as persons between the ages of 15 and 24.
4. Youth is defined as a social position that (reflect / reflects) the meanings given to individuals.
5. Youth is the stage of (constructing / constructs) the self-concept.

Questions

1. How does the UN define youth?

2. What different variables influence the self-concept?

Free Writing

Write about a memorable event from your childhood.

____

____

____

____

____

____

____

____

Cultural Spotlight: *Coming-of-Age Stories*

Coming-of-age stories focus on the growth of the protagonist from youth to adulthood. They usually focus on teenage life and are a very common genre for movies and novels in cultures around the world. The personal and emotional growth of the protagonist is usually an important characteristic of this genre.

It is undeniable that audiences around the world have a fascination with adolescence based on the number of movies and books focused on this stage of life. Some very famous and critically acclaimed coming-of-age novels include *Kamchatka* by Marcelo Figueras from Argentina, *Abigail* by Magda Szabó from Hungary, and *Persepolis* by Marjane Satrapi from Iran, among many others. In all of these novels, the reader is able to witness the protagonist's growth and development in the face of life's trials and tribulations.

On top of coming-of-age stories, audiences around the world are obsessed with youthful characters on screen. There is a natural fascination with stories about youth and what happens during this pivotal time of life. One famous example is the massively popular movie *Titanic*. This movie presents a part of history through the eyes of two attractive Hollywood stars.

In this movie, Brock Lovett and his team of treasure hunters search the wreck of RMS Titanic for a necklace with a rare diamond, the Heart of the Ocean in 1996. They recover a safe containing a drawing of a young woman wearing only the necklace dated April 14, 1912, the day the ship struck the iceberg. Rose Dawson Calvert, the woman in the drawing, is brought aboard and tells Lovett of her experiences on the *Titanic*.

In 1912, 17-year-old first-class passenger Rose DeWitt Bukater, her fiancé Cal

Hockley, and her mother Ruth board the luxurious *Titanic*. Ruth emphasizes that Rose's marriage will resolve their family's financial problems and allow them to retain their upper-class status. Distraught over the engagement, Rose climbs over the stern and contemplates suicide, but Jack Dawson, a poor artist, intervenes and discourages her.

Discovered with Jack, Rose tells a concerned Cal that she was peering over the edge and Jack saved her from falling. Cal becomes indifferent, and it is suggested to him that Jack be rewarded. He then invites Jack to dine with them in first-class. Jack and Rose develop a tentative friendship. Following dinner, Rose secretly joins Jack at a party in third-class.

Aware of Cal and Ruth's disapproval, Rose rebuffs Jack's advances, but later realizes she prefers him over Cal. After rendezvousing on the bow at sunset, Rose takes Jack to her room. She requests that he sketches her wearing Cal's engagement present, the Heart of the Ocean. On the forward deck, they witness the ship's collision with an iceberg. Cal discovers Jack's sketch of Rose and an insulting note from her in his safe along with the necklace. When Jack and Rose attempt to inform Cal of the collision, Cal retaliates by having someone slip the necklace into Jack's pocket, accusing him of theft. Jack is arrested and restrained in an office on board. Cal puts the necklace in his own coat pocket.

With the ship sinking, Rose flees Cal and her mother and frees Jack. On the boat deck, Cal and Jack encourage her to board a lifeboat. While intending only to save himself, Cal claims he can ensure he and Jack get off safely. As her lifeboat lowers, Rose realizes she cannot leave Jack, and jumps back on board. Cal gets a pistol and chases Rose and Jack into the flooding first-class dining saloon. After using up his ammunition, he relents. Cal realizes he gave his coat, and consequently the necklace, to Rose. He later boards a lifeboat by carrying a lost child.

After braving several obstacles, Jack and Rose return to the boat deck. The lifeboats have departed and passengers are falling to their deaths as the stern rises out of the water. The ship breaks in half, dropping the stern into the water. Jack and Rose climb onto the back of it, and ride it into the ocean. He helps her onto a wooden panel buoyant enough for only one person. He assures her that she will die an old woman, warm in her bed. Jack dies of hypothermia, but Rose is saved by a returning lifeboat. On board, Rose hides from Cal en route to New York City, where she gives her name as Rose Dawson. Rose says she later read that Cal committed suicide after losing his fortune in the Wall Street Crash of 1929.

Sentence Structure: ***Make sentences using the examples below.***

1. encourage ~ to

   ex) Jack encouraged her to board a lifeboat.

   ____

2. accuse ~ of

   ex) He accused him of theft.

   ____

3. critically acclaimed

   ex) Some very famous and critically acclaimed coming-of-age novels include···

   ____

Cultural Spotlight: Music

Listen and circle the correct words. (1)

My Heart Will Go On (Celine Dion)

Every night in my dreams
I see you, I (feel / fill) you
That is how I (no / know) you go on
(Per, Far) across the distance
And spaces between us
You have come to show you go on
Near, far, (whenever / wherever) you are
I believe that the heart does go on
Once more you open the door
  And you're here in my heart
And my heart will go on and on
Love can touch us one time
  And (cast / last) for a lifetime
And never (let / read) go 'til we're gone
Love was when I loved you
One true time I hold to
In my life we'll always go on
Near, far, (whenever / wherever) you are
I believe that the heart does go on
Once more you open the door
  And you're here in my heart
And my heart will go on and on
You're here, there's nothing I (fear / feel)
And I know that my heart will go on
  We'll stay forever this way
You are safe in my heart and
My heart will go on and on

Listen and circle the correct words. (2)

Youth (Troye Sivan)

What if...
What if we run away?
What if...
What if we (left / laughter) today?
What if we said goodbye to safe and sound?
What if...
What if we're hard to find?
What if...
What if we lost our minds?
What if we let them fall behind
And they're never found?

And when the (rights / lights) start flashing like a photo booth
And the stars exploding
We'll be fireproof
My youth
My youth is yours
Tripping on skies, (sipping / shipping) waterfalls

My youth
My youth is yours
Runaway now and forevermore
My youth
My youth is yours
A truth so loud you can't ignore
My youth, my youth, my youth
My youth is yours

What if...?
What if we start to drive?
What if...?
What if we close our eyes?
What if...?
Speeding through red (rights / lights) into paradise
Because we've no time for getting old
Mortal body, timeless souls
Cross your fingers, here we go

And when the lights start (flashing like / flash like) a photo booth
And the stars exploding
We'll be fireproof

My youth
My youth is yours
Tripping on skies, sipping waterfalls
My youth
My youth is yours
Runaway now and forevermore
My youth
My youth is yours
A truth so loud you can't ignore
My youth, my youth, my youth
My youth is yours

My youth is yours

Listen and fill in the blanks. (1)

My Heart Will Go On (Celine Dion)

Every night in my dreams
I see you, (   )
That is how (   ) you go on
(   ) the distance
And spaces between us
  You have come to show you go on
Near, far, (   )
I believe that the heart does go on
Once more you open the door
  And you're here in my heart
And my heart will go on and on
Love can touch us one time
  (   ) for a lifetime
And never (   ) 'til we're gone
Love was when I loved you
One true time I hold to
  In my life we'll always go on
Near, far, (   )
I believe that the heart does go on
Once more you open the door
  And you're here in my heart
And my heart will go on and on
You're here, there's nothing (   )
And I know that my heart will go on
We'll stay forever this way
You are safe in my heart and
My heart will go on and on

Listen and fill in the blanks. (2)

Youth (Troye Sivan)

What if...
What if we run away?
What if...
What if we left today?
What if we said goodbye to
(   )?
What if...
What if we're hard to find?
What if...
What if we lost our minds?
What if we let them
(   )
And they're never found?

And when the lights start flashing
like a photo booth
And the stars exploding
We'll be fireproof

My youth
My youth is yours
(   ), sipping waterfalls
My youth
My youth is yours
Runaway now and forevermore
My youth
My youth is yours
A truth so loud you can't ignore
My youth, my youth, my youth
My youth is yours

What if...?
What if we start to drive?
What if...?
What if we close our eyes?
What if...?
Speeding through red lights into
paradise
Because we've no time for getting old
Mortal body (   ) souls
Cross your fingers, here we go

And when the lights start
(   ) a photo booth
And the stars exploding
We'll be fireproof

My youth
My youth is yours
Tripping on skies, (   )
My youth
My youth is yours
Runaway now and forevermore
My youth
My youth is yours
A truth so loud you can't ignore
My youth, my youth, my youth
My youth is yours

My youth is yours

Wrap-Up

Share your opinions:

1. Do you think you have a high or low level of dependency on your parents?
2. Do you think you are an individualist or a collectivist?
3. Do you think it's better for young people to grow up in cities or the country?
4. Do you think young people have a better life now than they did in the past?
5. Can you think of any coming-of-age novels or movies?

Getting Older

Pros	Cons

UNIT 3
Marriage

TOPICS
- Wedding Traditions
- Love Stories

ICEBREAKERS
- Describe your ideal wedding.
- How are Korean weddings different from weddings in other countries?

Vocabulary Preview

A. *Matching*

1. implement (v.) _____
2. vary (v.) _____
3. intricately (adv.) _____
4. roughly (adv.) _____
5. medicinal (adj.) _____
6. calm (v.) _____
7. attire (n.) _____
8. harmonious (adj.) _____

a. in a very complicated or detailed manner
b. put a decision or plan into effect
c. having healing properties
d. pleasing; free from disagreement
e. differ in size, amount, degree, or nature
f. clothes
g. make someone tranquil and quiet; soothe
h. approximately

B. *Fill in the blanks using the vocabulary words above.*

1. The plan was not _______________ correctly.
2. There were _______________ 200 people at the conference.
3. Proper _______________ is required to enter the restaurant.
4. The meal had a _______________ combination of flavors.
5. The yoga retreat will _______________ your mind and body.
6. The cost of a room at this hotel _______________ with the season.
7. Ginseng is an important _______________ plant.
8. Occupation and income are _______________ linked to housing and settlement patterns.

Language Focus (Tenses)

Choose the best option to complete the following sentences.

1. I drove a car while I _______ music.

   a. listening   b. was listening to

   c. was listening at   d. listen to

2. The main conference room _______ in use since 8:00 a.m.

   a. have been   b. is

   c. was   d. has been

3. My father _______ at the company for over 20 years.

   a. was work   b. was worked

   c. had been worked   d. has been working

4. The country's department stores _______ total sales decline by 1.9 percent since 2013.

   a. have seen   b. had seen

   c. saw   d. was seen

5. Due to the late arrival of the keynote speaker, most of those in attendance _______ waiting at least 20 minutes when he finally arrived.

   a. had been   b. did

   c. has been   d. are

6. He _______ been here for more than 15 minutes before he excused himself and left the meeting.

   a. has   b. hasn't

   c. had not   d. had

7. The amount of fiscal responsibility _______ decreasing since the election.

   a. have been   b. has been

   c. didn't   d. will have been

Wedding Traditions

One of the most amazing things about our world is how the same action or tradition can be implemented so differently in each culture. Take marriage for instance; it's practiced around the world, but the way a wedding is celebrated varies immensely across cultures. Here are some of the many ways wedding traditions are different around the world.

Rather than wearing hand jewelry, in India it's traditional for the bride to spend hours getting *mehndi* intricately painted on her. *Mehndi* is paint made from henna. While it requires a lot of patience, the result is a beautiful work of art that lasts roughly two weeks on the skin. Interestingly enough, mehndi is actually painted onto the bride for its medicinal properties. It's meant to help calm the bride while dealing with the stress of the wedding day.

If you attend a wedding in Norway, you'll love the cake for two reasons. For starters, a traditional wedding cake, called a kransekake, is created by placing iced almond cake rings on top of each other to create a cone shape. Even better? In the center of this hollow cake, you'll find gifts like a bottle of champagne or wine. Another fun tradition is that the bride and groom pick up the top ring of the cake. It's a legend in Norway that however many layers stick to it underneath are the amount of children they will have.

Although it's common in many cultures for the bride to dance with various guests, in Cuba the dance comes with a price. Every man who dances with the bride is traditionally required to pin money to her dress. This custom is practiced to help the couple pay for the wedding and the honeymoon.

While still wearing their wedding attire, German newlyweds sometimes saw a log in half while all their guests watch in a tradition known as Baumstamm Sägen. The tradition is meant to symbolize how the couple will work together as they face obstacles in their marriage.

Following the wedding ceremony, Filipino newlyweds traditionally release two doves, one male and one female. The birds are meant to represent a harmonious life ahead for the couple. It's a peaceful show of love ahead for the newlyweds.

These examples just provide a small glimpse of the many beautiful wedding traditions around the world.

Reading Comprehension

Circle the correct words to complete the sentences.

1. The way a wedding is celebrated (vary / varies) immensely.
2. It's traditional for the bride to spend (hour / hours) getting ready.
3. The ginseng plant is used for its (medicine / medicinal) properties.
4. Every man who (dance / dances) with the bride is required to pin money to her dress.
5. German (newlywed / newlyweds) sometimes saw a log in half while all their guests watch.

Questions

1. What is mehndi? Why is it used?

2. Why do Cuban men pin money to the bride's dress?

Free Writing

Write about one wedding tradition in your country.

Cultural Spotlight: *Love Stories*

In the same way that audiences around the world are obsessed with attractive young characters, they also can't get enough of seeing these young characters involved in relationships. Love stories are truly ubiquitous in every culture and across all forms of entertainment. This obsession has been around for quite some time and one great example is the aptly named hit movie, *Love Story*.

In this movie, Oliver Barrett IV, the heir of an upper-class family, is attending Harvard where he plays ice hockey. He meets Jenny Cavilleri, a quick-witted, working-class Radcliffe College student of classical music. They quickly fall in love despite their differences.

When Jenny reveals her plans to study in Paris, Oliver is upset that he does not figure in those plans. He proposes, she accepts, and they travel to the Barrett mansion so that she can meet Oliver's parents, who are judgmental and unimpressed with her. Later Oliver's father tells him that he will cut him off financially if he marries Jenny. After graduation, Oliver and Jenny marry nonetheless.

Without his father's financial support, they struggle to pay Oliver's way through Harvard Law School while Jenny works as a teacher. Oliver graduates third in his class and takes a position at a respectable New York City law firm. They are ready to start a family, but fail to conceive. After many tests Oliver is told that Jenny is terminally ill.

Oliver attempts to live a "normal life" without telling Jenny of her condition, but she finds out after confronting her doctor. Oliver buys tickets to Paris, but she declines to go, wanting only to spend time with him. To pay for Jenny's cancer therapy, Oliver seeks money from his estranged father, who asks him if he has "gotten a girl in trouble." Oliver simply says yes, and his father writes a check.

From her hospital bed, Jenny makes funeral arrangements with her father, then asks for Oliver. She tells him to not blame himself, insisting that he never held her back from music and it was worth it for the love they shared. Jenny's last wish is made when she asks him to embrace her tightly before she dies. As a grief-stricken Oliver leaves the hospital, he sees his father outside, having rushed to New York City from Massachusetts as soon as he heard the news about Jenny and wanting to offer his help. Oliver tells him, "Jenny's dead," and his father says "I'm sorry," to which Oliver responds, "Love - Love means never having to say you're sorry", something that Jenny had said to him earlier.

Sentence Structure: ***Make sentences using the examples below.***

1. despite ~

   ex) They quickly fell in love despite their differences.

   ____

2. decline to ~

   ex) She declines to go there.

   ____

3. worth ~ing

   ex) The book was worth reading.

   ____

4. worth + (the) noun

   ex) It was worth the effort.

   ____

5. rush to ~

   ex) She rushed to New York City from Massachusetts.

   ____

Cultural Spotlight: Music

Listen and circle the correct words. (1)

Where Do I Begin? (Andy Williams)

Where do I begin
To tell the story of how great a love can be
The sweet love story that is older than the (see / sea)
The simple truth about the love she brings to me
Where do I start

With her first hello
She gave new meaning to this empty (word / world) of mine
There'd never be another love, another time
She came into my life and made the living fine
She fills my heart

She fills my heart (with / in) very special things
With angels' songs, with wild imaginings
She fills my soul with so much love
That anywhere I go I'm never lonely
With her around, who could be lonely
I reach for her hand, it's always there

How long does it last
Can love be measured by the hours in a day
I have no answers now but this much I can say
I know I'll need her 'till the stars all burn away
And she'll be there

How long does it last
Can love be measured by the hours in a day
I have no answers now but this much I can say
I know I'll need her 'till the stars all (burn away / burnt away)
And she'll be there

Listen and circle the correct words. (2)

Marry You (Bruno Mars)

It's a beautiful night, we're looking for something dumb to do
Hey baby, I think I wanna marry you
Is it the look (in / on) your eyes or is it this dancing juice?
Who cares, baby, I think I wanna marry you
Well, I know this little chapel on the boulevard we can go
No one will know, oh, come on girl
Who cares if we (trashed / 're trashed), got a pocket full of cash we can blow
Shots of patron and it's on, girl
Don't say no, no, no, no, no
Just say yeah, yeah, yeah, yeah, yeah
And we'll go, go, go, go, go
If you're ready, like I'm ready
'Cause it's a beautiful night, we're looking for something dumb to do
Hey baby, I think I wanna marry you
Is it the look in your eyes or is it this dancing juice?
Who cares, baby, I think I wanna marry you, oh
I'll go get a ring, let the (choir / quiet) bells sing like, ooh
So what ya wanna do? Let's just run, girl
If we wake up and you wanna break up, that's cool
No, I (want / won't) blame you, it was fun, girl
Don't say no no no no no
Just say yeah yeah yeah yeah yeah
And we'll go go go go go
If you're ready, like I'm ready
'Cause it's a beautiful night, we're looking for something dumb to do
Hey baby, I think I wanna marry you
Is it the look in your eyes, or is it this dancing juice?
Who cares baby, I think I wanna marry you
Just say I do
Tell me right now, baby
Tell me right now, baby, baby
Just say I do
Tell me right now, baby
Tell me right now, baby, baby
Oh It's a beautiful night, we're looking for something dumb to do
Hey baby, I think I wanna marry you
Is it the look in your eyes, or is it this dancing (shoes / juice)?
Who cares baby, I think I wanna marry you

Listen and fill in the blanks. (1)

Where Do I Begin? (Andy Williams)

Where do I begin
To tell the story of how great a love can be
The sweet love story that is older (   )
The simple truth about the love she brings to me
Where do I start

With her first hello
She gave new meaning to this (   ) of mine
There'd never be another love, another time
She came into my life and made the living fine
She fills my heart

She (   ) with very special things
With angels' songs, with wild imaginings
She fills my soul with so much love
That anywhere I go I'm never lonely
With her around, who could be lonely
I reach for her hand, it's always there

How long does it last
Can love be measured by the hours in a day
I have no answers now but this much I can say
I know I'll need her 'till the stars all burn away
And she'll be there

How long does it last
Can love be measured by the hours in a day
I have no answers now but this much I can say
I know I'll need her 'till the stars all (   )
And she'll be there

Listen and fill in the blanks. (2)

Marry You (Bruno Mars)

It's a beautiful night, we're looking for something (   )
Hey baby, I think I wanna marry you
Is it (   ) your eyes or is it this dancing juice?
Who cares, baby, I think I wanna marry you
Well, I know this little chapel on the boulevard we can go
No one will know, oh, come on girl
Who cares if (   ), got a pocket full of cash we can blow
Shots of patron and it's on, girl
Don't say no, no, no, no, no
Just say yeah, yeah, yeah, yeah, yeah
And we'll go, go, go, go, go
If you're ready, like I'm ready
'Cause it's a beautiful night, we're looking for something dumb to do
Hey baby, I think I wanna marry you
Is it the look in your eyes or is it this dancing juice?
Who cares, baby, I think I wanna marry you, oh
I'll go get a ring, let the (   ) sing like, ooh
So what ya wanna do? Let's just run, girl
If we wake up and you wanna break up, that's cool
No, I (   ), it was fun, girl
Don't say no no no no no
Just say yeah yeah yeah yeah yeah
And we'll go go go go go
If you're ready, like I'm ready
'Cause it's a beautiful night, we're looking for something dumb to do
Hey baby, I think I wanna marry you
Is it the look in your eyes, or is it this dancing juice?
Who cares baby, I think I wanna marry you
Just say I do
Tell me right now, baby
Tell me right now, baby, baby
Just say I do
Tell me right now, baby
Tell me right now, baby, baby
Oh It's a beautiful night, we're looking for something dumb to do
Hey baby, I think I wanna marry you
Is it the look in your eyes, or is it this dancing juice?
Who cares baby, I think I wanna marry you

Wrap-Up

Share your opinions:

1. What is the most famous love story in your country?
2. Do you think it's important to spend a lot of money on a wedding?
3. What do you think is the most interesting wedding tradition from this unit?
4. Do you know any other interesting wedding traditions from another country?
5. Do you think wedding traditions will change in your country in the future?

Love Stories

Pros	Cons

UNIT 4

Funerals

TOPICS

- Funeral Traditions
- The Supernatural

ICEBREAKERS

- What are some funeral traditions in your country?
- Do you like movies about supernatural beings?

Vocabulary Preview

A. *Matching*

1. ingrained (adj.) _____	a. noisy, energetic, and cheerful
2. prototypical (adj.) _____	b. purely in terms of what is being represented
3. boisterous (adj.) _____	c. firmly fixed or established
4. fuse (v.) _____	d. a hollow container
5. cathartic (adj.) _____	e. the first, original, or typical form of something
6. vessel (n.) _____	f. rich or luxurious
7. lavish (adj.) _____	g. providing psychological relief through the open expression of emotions
8. symbolically (adv.) _____	h. join or blend to form a single entity

B. *Fill in the blanks using the vocabulary words above.*

1. The _______________ crowd began cheering loudly after he scored the winning goal.
2. A pot is a _______________ for holding food.
3. It was a simple gesture, but _______________ important.
4. He has incredible arm strength. He has the _______________ physique for a pitcher.
5. Talking to a therapist is a _______________ process.
6. Everyone feels this way. These attitudes are very deeply _______________ in our culture.
7. She enjoys a very _______________ lifestyle and always goes shopping.
8. I will _______________ Mexican and French ingredients to create this unique meal.

Language Focus (Adjectives and Adverbs)

Choose the best option to complete the following sentences.

1. When someone becomes ill, they select the tree where they will _______ be entombed.

   a. eventually b. frequently
   c. emotionally d. approximate

2. Families save up for long periods of time to raise the resources for a _______ funeral.

   a. frugal b. lavish
   c. thrifty d. plain

3. Our competition has _______ prices to ours.

   a. comparatively b. comparable
   c. compared d. comparing

4. Voice phishing fraud is a crime which makes people _______.

   a. anxious b. anxiety
   c. anxiously d. anxiousness

5. The manager asked his employees to _______ evacuate the flooding office building.

   a. quickest b. quickly
   c. quicker d. quick

6. I am proud to say that our product _______ for use.

   a. is safe b. is safety
   c. is safely d. is safeness

7. Genetically modified chickens grow _______ as naturally raised chickens.

   a. twice biggest b. twice as bigger
   c. twice as biggest d. twice as big

Unique Funeral Traditions

Funeral practices are deeply ingrained in culture and the varied customs around the globe reflect a wide range of beliefs and values. Let's look at some funeral traditions that might strike outsiders as odd.

The New Orleans jazz funeral is one of the prototypical images of New Orleans, Louisiana. The boisterous, jazz-tinged funeral procession fuses West African, French, and African-American traditions. These funerals strike a unique balance between joy and grief as mourners are led by a marching band. The band plays sorrowful songs at first, but once the body is buried, they shift to an upbeat note. Cathartic dancing is generally a part of the event to commemorate the life of the deceased.

Many ethnic groups in the Philippines have unique funeral practices. The Benguet of the Northwestern Philippines blindfold their dead and place them next to the main entrance of a house. Their Tinguian neighbors dress bodies in their best clothes, sit them on a chair and place a lit cigarette in their mouth. The Caviteño, who live near Manila, bury their dead in a hollowed-out tree trunk. When someone becomes ill, they select the tree where they will eventually be entombed.

Many Vajrayana Buddhists in Mongolia and Tibet believe in the transmigration of spirits after death. This means that the soul moves on, while the body becomes an empty vessel. To return it to the earth, the body is chopped into pieces and placed on a mountaintop, which exposes it to the elements — including vultures. This sky *burial* is a practice that has been done for thousands of years and, according to a recent report, about 80% of Tibetans still choose this funeral type.

In Tana Toraja in eastern Indonesia, funerals are raucous affairs involving the whole village. They can last anywhere from days to weeks. Families save up for long periods of time to raise the resources for a lavish funeral, where sacrificial water buffalo will carry the deceased's soul to the afterlife. Until that moment, which can take place years after physical death, the dead relative is referred to simply as a "person who is sick," or even one "who is asleep." They are laid down in special rooms in the family home, where they are symbolically fed, cared for, and taken out; very much still a part of their relative's lives.

These unique funeral customs provide an interesting perspective on how different cultures view death and the afterlife.

Reading Comprehension

Circle the correct word to complete the sentence.

1. Funeral practices are (shallowly / deeply) ingrained in culture.
2. Funerals in New Orleans strike a unique balance between joy and grief as (mornings / mourners) are led by a marching band.
3. Many ethnic groups in the Philippines have (unique / basic) funeral practices.
4. In Tana Toraja, funerals are (quiet / raucous) affairs involving the whole village.
5. The body is placed on a mountaintop, which (exposes / exposing) it to the elements.

Questions

1. Describe a New Orleans jazz funeral.

2. What is a sky burial?

Free Writing

Do you know any other unique funeral traditions? Share one here.

Cultural Spotlight: *The Supernatural*

Since the beginning of recorded history, humans have had a fascination with the supernatural. The supernatural encompasses all entities, places and events that would fall outside the scope of the scientific understanding of the laws of nature. This includes entities which transcend the observable Universe, such as immaterial beings like angels, gods, and spirits. Spirits and ghosts are particularly prevalent in movies, novels, and TV shows. One great example is the popular movie *Ghost*.

In this movie, Sam Wheat and his girlfriend Molly Jensen renovate and move into an apartment in Manhattan with the help of Sam's friend and co-worker Carl Bruner. One afternoon, Sam confides in Carl his discovery of unusually high balances in obscure bank accounts. He decides to investigate the matter himself, declining Carl's offer of assistance. That night, Sam and Molly are attacked by a mugger who shoots and kills Sam in a scuffle before stealing his wallet. Sam sees Molly crying over his body and discovers he is now a ghost, invisible and unable to interact with the mortal world.

Molly is distraught in the days after Sam's death, as Sam remains close to her. Carl comes over and suggests Molly take a walk with him; Sam, unable to follow, stays behind. Moments later, the mugger enters the apartment in search of something. When Molly returns, Sam scares their cat into attacking the thug, who flees. Sam follows the mugger to his Brooklyn apartment and learns that the man, Willie Lopez, was sent by an unknown party.

After leaving Willie's residence, Sam happens upon the parlor of psychic Oda Mae Brown, a charlatan pretending to commune with spirits of the dead. She is shocked to discover her true psychic gift when she can hear Sam speaking. Sam persuades her to warn Molly that she is in danger. To allay Molly's skepticism, Oda Mae relays information that only Sam could know. Molly later gives Willie's address to Carl, who volunteers to investigate. She then goes to the police, who have no file for Willie but they show her Oda Mae's lengthy one as a forger and con artist.

Meanwhile, Sam follows Carl and is devastated to learn he and Willie are working together. Carl is laundering money for drug dealers and he had Willie rob Sam to get his apartment key. Carl uses the key to obtain Sam's book of passwords and transfers the money to a single account under the fictitious name Rita Miller.

Sam learns from a violent poltergeist haunting the subway system how to use energy to move objects. Sam then persuades Oda Mae to help him thwart Carl. Before Carl can transfer the money for his clients, Oda Mae impersonates Rita Miller, closes the account, and donates the $4 million to charity. As Carl desperately searches for the money, Sam reveals his presence by typing his name on the computer keyboard. Carl goes to Molly, who reveals she spotted Oda Mae closing an account at the bank. Carl and Willie go to Oda Mae's place but Sam warns her and her sisters to take shelter. When Willie arrives, Sam spooks him, causing him to flee into the street in a fit of panic before being struck and killed by an oncoming car. Shadowy demons emerge from the darkness to drag Willie's ghost down to Hell.

Sam and Oda Mae return to the apartment where, by levitating a penny into Molly's hand, he convinces Molly that Oda Mae is telling the truth about him. Oda Mae allows Sam to possess her body so he and Molly can share a slow dance. Carl breaks into the apartment but Sam is too exhausted from the possession to fight Carl. The women escape onto the fire escape, to a loft under construction, but Carl catches Oda Mae and holds her at gunpoint, demanding the check. Sam recovers and pushes Carl off her, prompting Carl to take Molly hostage and plead with Sam for the check. Sam disarms Carl and attacks him again. Carl tries to escape through a window and tosses a suspended hook at Sam, but the hook swings back, shattering the window and causing it to slide down, fatally impaling Carl with a glass shard. The shadowy demons who came for Willie return to claim Carl's ghost for Hell.

Sam asks if the women are okay. Molly is now able to hear him and a heavenly light shines in the room, illuminating Sam's presence. Realizing that it is time for him to go with his task now completed, he and Molly share a tearful goodbye and one final kiss, finally having proper closure between them. Sam thanks Oda Mae for her help and then walks into the light and onward to Heaven.

Sentence Structure: *Make sentences using the examples below.*

1. in search of ~

   ex) The mugger enters the apartment in search of something.

   ____

2. cause ~ to ~

   ex) What caused him to act like that?

   ____

3. happen upon

   ex) After leaving Willie's residence, Sam happens upon the parlor of psychic Oda Mae Brown.

   ____

Cultural Spotlight: Music

Listen and circle the correct words. (1)

Unchained Melody (Righteous Brothers)

Woah, my love, my darling
I've hungered for your touch
A long, lonely time
And time goes (by / buy) so slowly
And time can do so much
Are you still mine?
I need your love
I need your love
God speed your love to me
Lonely rivers (flow / flaw)
To the sea, to the sea
To the open arms of the sea, yeah

Lonely rivers sigh
"Wait for me, wait for me"
I'll be coming home, wait for me

Woah, my love, my darling
I've hungered, hungered for your touch
A long, lonely time
And time goes by so slowly
And time can do so much
Are you still mine?
I need your love
I need your love
God speed your love to me

Listen and circle the correct words. (2)

See You Again (Wiz Khalifa)

It's been a long day without you, my friend
And I'll tell you all about it when I see you again
We've come a (long / wrong) way from where we began
Oh I'll tell you all about it when I see you again
When I see you again
Damn, who knew?
All the planes we flew, good things we been through
That I'd be standing right here talking to you
'Bout another path, I know we loved to (hit / heat) the road and laugh
But something told me that it wouldn't last
Had to switch up, look at things different, see the bigger picture
Those were the days, hard work forever pays
Now I see you in a better place
Uh
How can we not talk about family when family's all that we got?
Everything I went through, you were standing there by my side
And now you gon' be with me for the last ride
It's been a long day without you, my friend
And I'll tell you all about it when I see you again
We've come a long way from where we began
Oh I'll tell you all about it when I see you again
When I see you again
First, you both go out your (way / weigh) and the vibe is feeling strong
And what's small turned to a friendship, a friendship turned to a bond
And that bond will never be broken, the love will never get lost
(The love will never get lost)
And when brotherhood come first, then the line will never be crossed
Established it on our own when that line had to be drawn
And that line is what we reached, so remember me when I'm gone
(Remember me when I'm gone)
How can we not talk about family when family's all that we got?
Everything I went through you were standing there by my side
And now you gon' be with me for the last (ride / right)
So let the light guide your way, yeah
Hold every memory as you go
And every road you take
Will always lead you home, home

Listen and fill in the blanks. (1)

Unchained Melody (Righteous Brothers)

Woah, my love, my darling
I've hungered for your touch
A long, lonely time
And (   ) so slowly
And time can do so much
Are you still mine?
I need your love
I need your love
God speed your love to me

Lonely (   )
To the sea, to the sea
To the open arms of the sea, yeah
Lonely rivers sigh
"Wait for me, wait for me"
I'll be coming home, wait for me

Woah, my love, my darling
I've hungered, hungered for your touch
A long, lonely time
And (   ) so slowly
And time can do so much
Are you still mine?
I need your love
I need your love
God speed your love to me

Listen and fill in the blanks. (2)

See You Again (Wiz Khalifa)

It's been a long day without you, my friend
And I'll tell you all about it when I see you again
We've come a long way from where we began
Oh I'll tell you all about it when I see you again
When I see you again
Damn, who knew?
All the planes (   ), good things we been through
That I'd be standing right here talking to you
'Bout another path, I know we loved to hit the road and laugh
But something told me that it wouldn't last
Had to switch up, look at things different, see the bigger picture
Those were the days, hard work forever pays
Now I see you in a better place
Uh
How can we not talk about family when family's all that we got?
Everything I went through, you were standing there by my side
And now you gon' be with me for the last ride
It's been a long day without you, my friend
And I'll tell you all about it when I see you again
We've come a long way from where we began
Oh I'll tell you all about it when I see you again
When I see you again
First, you both go out your way and the vibe is feeling strong
And what's small turned to a friendship, a friendship turned to a bond
And that bond will never be broken, the love will never get lost
(The love will never get lost)
And when brotherhood come first, then the line will never
(   )
Established it on our own when that line had to be drawn
And that line is what we reached, so remember me when I'm gone
(Remember me when I'm gone)
How can we not talk about family when family's all that we got?
Everything I went through you were standing there by my side
And now you gon' be with me for the last ride
So (   ) your way, yeah
Hold every memory as you go
And every road you take
Will always lead you home, home

Wrap-Up

Share your opinions:

1. What do you think is the most interesting funeral tradition from this unit?
2. Do you like the idea of an upbeat funeral?
3. What are some unique traditions in your country?
4. Do you think it's important to keep traditions? Why or why not?
5. Can you think of any supernatural movies in your country?

Supernatural Movies

Pros	Cons

UNIT 5
Religion

TOPICS

- Geographical Differences
- Religious Discrimination

ICEBREAKERS

- Do you think your country is becoming more or less religious?
- What are the largest religions in your country?

Vocabulary Preview

A. *Matching*

1. demographic (n.) _____	a. having a large population
2. affiliation (n.) _____	b. a particular sector of a population
3. geographical (adj.) _____	c. lower in rank or status
4. adherents (n.) _____	d. forming an unbroken whole
5. populous (adj.) _____	e. relating to the physical features of an area
6. indigenous (adj.) _____	f. someone who supports a particular party, person, or set of ideas
7. inferior (adj.) _____	g. originating in a particular place; native
8. continuous (adj.) _____	h. the state or process of connecting or joining

B. *Fill in the blanks using the vocabulary words above.*

1. The town's ________________ suggest that the restaurant will do well there.
2. China is the world's most ________________ country.
3. These products are ________________ to the ones we bought last year.
4. Differences among ages and ________________ regions were assessed with the test.
5. My computer makes a ________________ buzzing sound.
6. She has been an ________________ of the Republican Party for a long time.
7. Are there any frog species ________________ to the area?
8. He says he is not sure which candidate to vote for and has no political ________________.

Language Focus (Comparisons)

Choose the best option to complete the following sentences.

1. Geography is important in religion. Asia-Pacific is the ______ region in the world.
   - a. populated
   - b. more populous
   - c. most populous
   - d. populating

2. Hong may be summoned for questions ______ this weekend.
   - a. as early as
   - b. as earlier as
   - c. more earlier
   - d. as earliest as

3. Consumers find shopping on the web far ______ than shopping at huge retailers.
   - a. more convenient
   - b. more conveniently
   - c. convenient
   - d. more convenienter

4. The world is ______ sustainable now than 40 years ago.
   - a. less
   - b. little
   - c. least
   - d. a little

5. The accident injured ______ 300 people.
   - a. more than
   - b. much than
   - c. the most than
   - d. many than

6. I find that the more education a person gets the ______ friendly they act towards needy people.
   - a. most
   - b. more
   - c. little
   - d. not

7. I believe that through volunteering, we can create the ______ place on Earth.
   - a. happier
   - b. happiest
   - c. happy
   - d. more happy

Religious Demographics and Discrimination

If you think religion belongs to the past and we live in a new age, you need to check out the facts: 84% of the world's population identifies with a religious group. Members of this demographic are generally younger and produce more children than those with no religious affiliation. This means the world is getting more religious, not less - although there are significant geographical variations.

According to 2015 figures, Christians form the biggest religious group by some margin, with 2.3 billion adherents or 31.2% of the total world population of 7.3 billion. Next come Muslims, with 1.8 billion followers (24.1%), Hindus with 1.1 billion (15.1%), and Buddhists with 500 million, or 6.9% of the total population.

Geography plays an important role in religion. Asia is the most populous region in the world, and also the most religious. It is home to 99% of Hindus, 99% of Buddhists, and 90% of those practicing folk or traditional religions. The region also hosts 76% of the world's religiously unaffiliated people, 700 million of whom are Chinese. Religion in Africa is also multifaceted and, as the world's second most populous continent, there are a lot of followers of multiple religions. The continent's various populations are mostly adherents of Christianity, Islam, and traditional African religions. South America is predominantly Catholic, North America is predominantly Christian, and Europe is a mix of Christianity, Islam and other religions.

It is no secret that religion has caused conflicts in the past and sadly, this shows no signs of stopping in the future. These conflicts have turned deadly in many instances and seem to be difficult to prevent. Religious beliefs and conflicts are simply too deep to be solved with any simple fix. This can spill over into daily life and rear its head as the age-old problem of religious discrimination.

Religious discrimination means treating people or groups differently because of what they do or do not believe in. One clear example still persisting to this day is the fact that indigenous populations around the world have dealt with continuous discrimination at the hands of occupying forces. In many instances, their beliefs were marginalized and considered inferior.

One major challenge facing governments around the world today is figuring out a way to prevent religious conflicts and religious discrimination.

Reading Comprehension

Circle the correct words to complete the sentences.

1. 84% of the world's population (identifies / identifying) with a religious group.
2. Members of the religious (demographical / demographic) are generally younger.
3. Christians (from / form) the biggest religious group by some margin.
4. Asia is the (least / most) populous region in the world.
5. One major challenge facing governments around the world today is (figure / figuring) out a way to prevent religious conflicts.

Questions

1. Which religions are predominantly found in Asia?

2. What is religious discrimination?

Free Writing

Do you think the religious population will increase or decrease in your country in the next decade? Explain your opinion.

Cultural Spotlight: *Religious Holidays*

Religions around the world have unique holidays in order to honor their beliefs. From the Islamic holiday of *Eid* to the Buddhist holiday of *Buddha's Birthday*, there are a number of different ways to celebrate. One of the most recognizable religious holidays around the world is the Christian holiday of *Christmas*, which commemorates the birth of Jesus. Over time, a famous character has become synonymous with Christmas. Let's take a closer look at Santa Claus and his origins.

Santa Claus, also known as *Father Christmas, Saint Nicholas, Saint Nick, Kris Kringle,* or simply *Santa*, is a legendary character originating in Western Christian culture who is said to bring gifts to the homes of well-behaved children and coal to naughty kids on Christmas Eve. The modern character of Santa Claus was based on traditions surrounding the historical *Saint Nicholas*, the British figure of *Father Christmas*, and the Dutch figure of *Sinterklaas*. Some maintain Santa Claus also absorbed elements of the Germanic deity Wodan, who was associated with the pagan midwinter event of Yule and led the Wild Hunt, a ghostly procession through the sky.

Santa Claus is generally depicted as a portly, jolly, white-bearded man wearing a red coat with a white fur collar and cuffs, red trousers, a red hat with white fur, and a black leather belt and boots, carrying a bag full of gifts for children. This image became popular in the United States and Canada in the 19th century due to the significant influence of the 1823 poem *A Visit from St. Nicholas*. Caricaturist and political cartoonist Thomas Nast also played a role in the creation of Santa's image. This image has been maintained and reinforced through song, radio, television, children's books, films, and advertising.

In modern folklore, Santa Claus is said to make lists of children throughout the world. He categorizes them according to their behavior. He then sets out to deliver presents, including toys and candy, to all of the well-behaved children in the world. Misbehaving children receive coal on the night of Christmas Eve. Santa Claus is said to accomplish this feat with the aid of his elves, who make the toys in his workshop at the North Pole. His flying reindeer are also said to provide assistance by pulling his sleigh. He is commonly portrayed as living at the North Pole, and laughing in a way that sounds like "ho ho ho."

Sentence Structure: ***Make sentences using the examples below.***

1. known as ~

   ex) Santa Claus, known as Saint Nicholas, is a legendary character.

   ____

2. be based on ~

   ex) The modern character of Santa Claus was based on traditions.

   ____

3. according to ~

   ex) He categorizes them according to their behavior.

   ____

4. deliver ~ to ~

   ex) He delivered presents to all of the well-behaved children in the world.

   ____

5. on the night of ~

   ex) Misbehaving children receive coal on the night of Christmas Eve.

   ____

6. said to ~

   ex) His flying reindeer are also said to provide assistance by pulling his sleigh.

   ____

Cultural Spotlight: Music

Listen and circle the correct words. (1)

Last Christmas (Wham!)

Last Christmas I gave you my heart
But the very next day you gave it away
This year, to (safe / save) me from tears
I'll give it to someone special

Once bitten and twice shy
I keep my distance, but you still catch my eye
Tell me baby, do you recognize me?
Well, it's been a year, it doesn't surprise me

"Merry Christmas" I wrapped it up and sent it
With a note saying "I love you", I (mean / meant) it
Now I know what a fool I've been
But if you kissed me now, I know you'd fool me again

Ohh
Oh, oh, baby

A (crowded / crowding) room, friends with tired eyes
I'm hiding from you and your soul of ice
My God, I thought you were someone to rely on
Me? I guess I was a shoulder to cry on

A face on a lover with a fire in his heart
A man under cover but you tore me apart
Ooh, ooh, now I've found a real love
You'll never (full / fool) me again

A face on a lover with a fire in his heart (I gave you mine)
A man under cover but you tore him apart
Maybe next year we'll give it to someone
I'll give it to someone special
Special
So long...

Listen and circle the correct words. (2)

All I Want for Christmas Is You (Mariah Carey)

I don't want a lot for Christmas
There is just one thing I need
I don't care about the (presents / pleasant)
Underneath the Christmas tree

I just want you for my own
More than you could ever know
Make my wish come true
All I want for Christmas is you, yeah

I don't want a lot for Christmas
There is just one thing I need
And I don't care about the presents
Underneath the Christmas tree

I don't need to hang my stocking
There upon the fireplace
Santa Claus won't make me happy
With a toy (in / on) Christmas Day

I just want you for my own
More than you could ever know
Make my wish come true
All I want for Christmas is you
You, baby

Oh, I won't ask (on / for) much this Christmas
I won't even wish for snow
And I'm just gonna keep on waiting
Underneath the mistletoe

I won't make a list and send it
To the North Pole for Saint Nick
I won't even stay awake to
Hear those magic reindeer click

'Cause I just want you here tonight
Holding on to me so (tide, tight)
What more can I do?
Baby, all I want for Christmas is you
You, baby

Oh, all the lights are shining so brightly everywhere
And the sound of children's laughter
(peels / fills) the air

And everyone is singing
I hear those sleigh bells ringing
Santa, won't you bring me the one I really need?
Won't you please bring my baby to me?

Oh, I don't want a lot for Christmas
This is all I'm asking for
I just wanna see my baby
Standing right (outside / inside) my door

Oh, I just want you for my own
More than you could ever know
Make my wish come true
Baby, all I want for Christmas... is you
You, baby

All I want for Christmas is you, baby
All I want for Christmas is you, baby
All I want for Christmas is you, baby
All I want for Christmas is you, baby
All I want for Christmas is you, baby

Listen and fill in the blanks. (1)

Last Christmas (Wham!)

Last Christmas I gave you my heart
But the very next day you (   )
This year, to save me (   )
I'll give it to someone special

Once bitten and twice shy
I keep my distance, but you still catch my eye
Tell me baby, do you recognize me?
Well, it's been a year, it doesn't surprise me

"Merry Christmas" I wrapped it up and sent it
With a note saying "I love you", I meant it
Now I know what a fool I've been
But if you kissed me now, I know you'd (   ) again

Ohh
Oh, oh, baby

A (   ), friends with tired eyes
I'm hiding from you and your soul of ice
My God, I thought you were someone to rely on
Me? I guess I was a shoulder to cry on

A face on a lover with a fire in his heart
A man under cover but you (   )
Ooh, ooh, now I've found a real love
You'll never fool me again

A face on a lover with a fire in his heart (I gave you mine)
A man under cover but you tore him apart
Maybe next year we'll give it to someone
I'll give it to someone special
Special
So long...

Listen and fill in the blanks. (2)

All I Want for Christmas Is You (Mariah Carey)

I don't want a lot for Christmas
There is just one thing I need
I don't (   )
Underneath the Christmas tree

I just want you for my own
More than you could ever know
(   )
All I want for Christmas is you, yeah

I don't want a lot for Christmas
There is just one thing I need
And I don't care about the presents
Underneath the Christmas tree

I don't need (   ) my stocking
There upon the fireplace
Santa Claus won't make me happy
With a toy on Christmas Day

I just want you for my own
More than you could ever know
Make my wish come true
All I want for Christmas is you
You, baby

Oh, I won't ask for much this Christmas

I won't even wish for snow
And I'm just gonna keep on waiting
Underneath the mistletoe
I won't make a list and send it
To the North Pole for Saint Nick
I won't even stay awake to
Hear those magic (   ) click

'Cause I just want you here tonight
Holding on to me so tight
What more can I do?
Baby, all I want for Christmas is you
You, baby

Oh, all the lights are shining so brightly everywhere
And the sound of children's laughter fills the air

And everyone is singing
I hear those (   ) bells ringing
Santa, won't you bring me the one I really need?
Won't you please bring my baby to me?

Oh, I don't want a lot for Christmas
This is all I'm asking for
I just wanna see my baby
Standing right outside my door

Oh, I just want you for my own
More than you could ever know
Make my wish come true
Baby, all I want for Christmas... is you
You, baby
All I want for Christmas is you, baby

All I want for Christmas is you, baby
All I want for Christmas is you, baby
All I want for Christmas is you, baby
All I want for Christmas is you, baby

Wrap-Up

Share your opinions:

1. Which part of the world do you think will see the largest increase in religion?
2. Which part of the world do you think will see the largest decrease in religion?
3. Do you think teachers should talk about religion in the classroom?
4. Do you celebrate any religious holidays?
5. Can you think of any other religious characters like Santa Claus?

Religious Holidays

Pros	Cons

UNIT 6
Countercultures

TOPICS
- Protests
- Pacifism

ICEBREAKERS
- Have you ever heard of hippies? What do you know about them?
- Have you ever seen a protest? What was it for?

Vocabulary Preview

A. *Matching*

1. pacifism (n.) _____	a. Not based on or conforming to what is generally done or believed
2. imply (v.) _____	b. A limiting condition or measure
3. unconventional (adj.) _____	c. Adopt or support a cause, belief, or way of life
4. beard (n.) _____	d. Most important, powerful, or influential
5. espouse (v.) _____	e. The belief that any violence is unjustifiable, and all disputes should be settled peacefully
6. dominant (adj.) _____	f. Having a willingness to act dishonestly for money
7. restriction (n.) _____	g. Facial hair
8. corrupt (adj.) _____	h. Strongly suggest the truth of something not expressly stated

B. *Fill in the blanks using the vocabulary words above.*

1. This ________________ does not apply to you. You are free to do whatever you want.
2. He hasn't shaved for five months. His ________________ is getting massive.
3. That company is under investigation for ________________ practices.
4. Due to his ________________, Tom would never consider joining the military since it went against his beliefs about violence.
5. The ________________ male gorilla is the largest in the group.
6. How could she ________________ that I was lying?
7. Most teachers ________________ the benefits to be gained from educational software.
8. She has ________________ work habits as she likes to work all night and sleep all day.

Language Focus (Relative Pronouns)

Choose the words that best complete the following sentences.

1. The Hippies were members of a counterculture group ______ began in the USA.
   a. what　　b. that
   c. whose　　d. whom

2. A counterculture is a group of people ______ behavior and values differ substantially from mainstream society.
   a. who　　b. whose
   c. that　　d. whom

3. Hippies are people ______ behavior, dress, worldviews, tastes in art, and music imply a rejection of conventional middle-class values.
   a. who　　b. whose
   c. that　　d. whom

4. A friend ______ I can have good conversations with is important to me.
   a. which　　b. whose
   c. what　　d. whom

5. Did you know that the new girl, ______ started in the office last week, is actually our manager's niece?
   a. who　　b. which
   c. whom　　d. that

6. The computer, ______ I bought last week, is already broken.
   a. whom　　b. who
   c. which　　d. when

7. It is difficult to determine ______ claims are true.
   a. that　　b. which
   c. who　　d. whom

The Hippies

A counterculture is a group of people whose behavior and values differ substantially from mainstream society. Members of countercultures are often shunned by their families and the communities they live in. Despite these difficulties, countercultures have worked to bring about a lot of important social changes throughout history.

Countercultures exist in every society around the world. Let's take a look at one of the most famous countercultures throughout history. The hippie movement began in the United States during the Vietnam War in the 1960s. Hippies are people whose behavior, dress, worldviews, tastes in art, and music imply a rejection of conventional middle-class values.

Hippies developed their own distinctive lifestyle. They favored long hair and casual, often unconventional, dress. Many males grew beards, and both men and women wore sandals and beads. Hippies advocated nonviolence and love. They promoted openness and tolerance as alternatives to the restrictions they felt were prevalent at the time.

Hippie fashion and values had a major effect on culture, influencing popular music, television, film, literature, and the arts. Since the 1960s, mainstream society has assimilated many aspects of hippie culture. The religious and cultural diversity the hippies espoused has gained widespread acceptance, and their pop versions of Eastern philosophy have reached a larger audience.

One important aspect of hippie culture in the 1960s was protesting the Vietnam War. Most hippies considered themselves pacifists and did not want to participate in any wars, especially one they did not support. They perceived the dominant culture as corrupt.

Hippies used alternative arts, street theatre, and folk music as a way of expressing their feelings, their protests and their vision of the world. Hippies opposed political orthodoxy, choosing a gentle ideology that favored peace, love and personal freedom. An example of this mindset is expressed in The Beatles' famous song "All You Need is Love." By 1965, hippies had become an established social group, and the movement eventually expanded around the world.

Reading Comprehension

Circle the correct words to complete the sentences.

1. The hippie movement (started / ended) in the 1960s.
2. Hippies (accepted / rejected) conventional values.
3. Hippies (supported / opposed) tolerance.
4. Most male hippies had very (neat / long) facial hair.
5. The hippies were (for / against) the Vietnam War.

Questions

1. Why were hippies described as pacifists? Provide an example to support your answer.

2. Describe hippie fashion. How did they dress?

Free Writing

What do you think about hippies? Write a short paragraph explaining your opinion.

Cultural Spotlight: *Countercultures Become Mainstream*

Sometimes countercultures become so popular they drift into mainstream society. A perfect example is the hippie movement of the 1960s from this unit's reading. This started as a small grassroots movement and grew to become known around the world. The popular movie *Forrest Gump* does a great job of capturing the hippie movement and its relevance to mainstream society.

This movie starts in 1981, at a bus stop in Georgia, when a man named Forrest Gump recounts his life story to strangers who sit next to him on a bench. In 1951, in Alabama, young Forrest is fitted with leg braces to correct a curved spine, and is unable to walk properly. He lives alone with his mother, who runs a boarding house out of their home that attracts many tenants, including a young Elvis Presley, who plays the guitar for Forrest and incorporates Forrest's jerky dance movements into his performances. On his first day of school, Forrest meets a girl named Jenny Curran, and the two become best friends.

Forrest is often bullied because of his physical disability and marginal intelligence. While fleeing from several bullies, his leg braces break off, revealing Forrest to be a very fast runner. This talent eventually allows him to receive a football scholarship at the University of Alabama in 1963. He witnesses Governor George Wallace's stand in the schoolhouse door at which he returns a dropped book to Vivian Malone Jones, becomes a top kick returner, is named on the All-American team, and meets President John F. Kennedy at the White House.

After graduating college in 1967, Forrest enlists in the U.S. Army. During basic training, he befriends a fellow soldier nicknamed Bubba, who convinces Forrest to go into the shrimping business with him after their service. In 1968, they are sent to Vietnam. After months of routine operations, their platoon is ambushed while on patrol and Bubba is killed in action. Forrest saves several wounded platoon-mates, including his lieutenant, Dan Taylor, who loses both his legs—and is awarded the Medal of Honor for his heroism by President Lyndon B. Johnson.

At the anti-war "March on the Pentagon" rally, Forrest briefly reunites with Jenny, who has been living a hippie lifestyle. He also develops a talent for ping-pong, and becomes a sports celebrity as he competes against Chinese teams in ping-pong diplomacy, earning him an interview alongside John Lennon on *The Dick Cavett Show*. He spends the holidays and the 1972 new year in New York City with Lieutenant Dan, who has become an embittered handicap. Forrest soon meets President Richard Nixon and is put up in the Watergate complex, where he accidentally witnesses and reports some men with flashlights in the building keeping him awake. Forrest is eventually discharged from the army.

Returning to Alabama, Forrest endorses a company that makes ping-pong paddles. He uses the earnings to buy a shrimping boat in Bayou La Batre, fulfilling his promise to Bubba. Lieutenant Dan joins Forrest in 1974, and they initially have little success. After their boat becomes the only one to survive Hurricane Carmen, they pull in huge amounts of shrimp and create the Bubba Gump Shrimp Company, after which Lieutenant Dan finally thanks Forrest for saving his life. Lieutenant Dan invests into what Forrest thinks is "some kind of fruit company" and the two become millionaires, but Forrest also gives half of the earnings to Bubba's family. Forrest then returns home to see his mother as she dies of cancer.

In 1976, Jenny—in the midst of recovering from years of drugs and abuse—returns to visit Forrest, and after a while he proposes to her. That night she tells Forrest she loves him and the two make love, but she leaves the next morning. Heartbroken, Forrest goes running, and spends the next three years in a relentless cross-country marathon, becoming famous again. He eventually decides that he's grown tired of running (metaphorically and physically) and returns home to Alabama.

Back in 1981, Forrest reveals that he is waiting at the bus stop because he received a letter from Jenny, who asked him to visit her. As Forrest is finally reunited with Jenny, she introduces him to their son, named Forrest Gump, Jr. Jenny tells Forrest she is sick with an unknown disease, and the three move back to Alabama. Jenny and Forrest finally marry, but she dies a year later. The film ends with Forrest seeing his son off on his first day of school.

Sentence Structure: ***Make sentences using the examples below.***

1. die of ~

   ex) She died of cancer.

   ____

2. be sick with

   ex) She is sick with an unknown disease.

   ____

3. grow tired of

   ex) He eventually decides that he has grown tired of running and returns home.

   ____

Cultural Spotlight: Music

Listen and circle the correct words. (1)

Revolution (The Beatles)

Take two
Okay
You say you want a revolution
Well, you know
We all want to change the world
You tell me that it's (evolution / revolution)
Well, you know
We all want to change the world
But when you talk about (description / destruction)
Don't you know that you can count me out (in)
Don't you know it's gonna be
All right?
Don't you know it's gonna be (all right)
Don't you know it's gonna be (all right)
You say you got a real (solution / pollution)
Well, you know
We'd all love to see the plan
You ask me for a contribution
Well, you know
We're all doing what we can
But if you want money for people with minds that hate
All I can tell you is brother you have to wait
Don't you know it's gonna be (all right)
Don't you know it's gonna be (all right)
Don't you know it's gonna be (all right)
You say you'll change the (constitution / construction)
Well, you know
We'd all love to change your head
You tell me it's the institution
Well, you know
You better free your mind instead
But if you go carrying pictures of Chairman Mao
You ain't going to make it with anyone (anyway / anyhow)
Don't you know it's gonna be (all right)
Don't you know it's gonna be (all right)
Don't you know it's gonna be (all right)
All, all, all, all, all, all, all, all, all, all, all right

Listen and circle the correct words. (2)

San Francisco (Scott McKenzie)

If you're going to San Francisco
Be sure to (wear / where) some flowers in your hair
If you're going to San Francisco
You're gonna (meat / meet) some gentle people there

For those who come to San Francisco
Summertime will be a (loving / love-in) there
In the streets of San Francisco
Gentle people with flowers in their hair

All across the nation
Such a strange vibration
People in motion

There's a (hole / whole) generation
With a new explanation
People in motion
People in motion

For those who come to San Francisco
Be sure to (wear / where) some flowers in your hair
If you come to San Francisco
Summertime will be a love-in there

If you come to San Francisco
Summertime will be a love-in there

Listen and fill in the blanks. (1)

Revolution (The Beatles)

Take two
Okay
You say you (   )
Well, you know
We all want to change the world
You tell me that it's evolution
Well, you know
We all want to change the world
But when you (   )
Don't you know that you can count me out (in)
Don't you know it's gonna be
All right?
Don't you know it's gonna be (all right)
Don't you know it's gonna be (all right)
You say you got a real solution
Well, you know
We'd all love to see the plan
You ask me (   )
Well, you know
We're all doing what we can
But if you want money for people with minds that hate
All I can tell you is brother you have to wait
Don't you know it's gonna be (all right)
Don't you know it's gonna be (all right)
Don't you know it's gonna be (all right)
You say you'll change the constitution
Well, you know
We'd all love to change your head
You tell me (   )
Well, you know
You better free your mind instead
But if you go carrying pictures of Chairman Mao
You ain't going to make it with anyone anyhow
Don't you know it's gonna be (all right)
Don't you know it's gonna be (all right)
Don't you know it's gonna be (all right)
All, all, all, all, all, all, all, all, all, all, all right

Listen and fill in the blanks. (2)

San Francisco (Scott McKenzie)

If you're going to San Francisco
Be sure to ( ) in your hair
If you're going to San Francisco
You're gonna ( ) there

For those who come to San Francisco
Summertime will be a ( )
In the streets of San Francisco
Gentle people with flowers in their hair

All across the nation
Such a strange vibration
People in motion

There's a ( )
With a new explanation
People in motion
People in motion

For those who come to San Francisco
Be sure to wear some flowers ( )
If you come to San Francisco
Summertime will be a love-in there

If you come to San Francisco
Summertime will be a love-in there

Wrap-Up

Share your opinions:

1. Would you be a hippie if you were alive in the 1960s? Why?

2. Do you like hippie fashion? Why?

3. Do you like hippie music? Why?

4. Have you ever participated in a protest? What was it for?

5. Can you think of another counterculture that became mainstream?

Countercultures

Pros	Cons

Trending Topics

CHAPTER 2

Social Issues

Trending
Topics

UNIT 1
Social Division

TOPICS

- Economic Inequality
- Rags-to-Riches Stories

ICEBREAKERS

- Do you think there is a wealth gap in your country?
- What are some problems caused by economic inequality?

Vocabulary Preview

A. *Matching*

1. inequality (n.) _____	a. the action of sharing something with a number of recipients
2. distribution (n.) _____	b. arrive at an opinion by reasoning
3. poverty (n.) _____	c. a house and its occupants
4. enhance (v.) _____	d. a fact or situation that is observed to exist or happen
5. conclude (v.) _____	e. the quality of being unequal or uneven
6. household (n.) _____	f. each of the 100 equal groups into which a population can be divided
7. phenomenon (n.) _____	g. improve the quality, intensify, or increase
8. percentile (n.) _____	h. the state of being extremely poor

B. *Fill in the blanks using the vocabulary words above.*

1. A graduate degree is a great way to _______________ your skills.
2. Two million people in the country live in _______________ and struggle to find their next meal.
3. By the 1960s, most _______________ had a TV.
4. That score puts you in the 96th _______________.
5. They aimed for a more even _______________ of resources.
6. Gravity is a natural _______________.
7. Analysts _______________ that the stock will go up.
8. Global _______________ leads to increasing political and economic problems.

Language Focus (Conjunctions and Prepositions)

Choose the best option to complete the following sentences.

1. In 1820, the ratio ______ the income of the top and bottom 20 percent of the world's population was three to one.

    a. between　　b. with
    c. during　　d. by

2. ______ the possibility of rain tomorrow, the event will go ahead as planned.

    a. Despite　　b. While
    c. Aside　　d. Although

3. The scheduled presentation for today has been postponed ______ next Friday.

    a. by　　b. until
    c. still　　d. ago

4. She spent 20 million won on hotel bills ______ repairing her house.

    a. about　　b. while
    c. during　　d. while she

5. The merger documents need to be ______ the corporate office by the end of business hours today.

    a. on　　b. from
    c. with　　d. at

6. ______ the construction on the building has finished, there will be much less traffic congestion.

    a. Due to　　b. Usually
    c. Regarding　　d. Now that

7. Nobody will be allowed inside this building ______ accompanied by a security guard.

    a. once　　b. although
    c. unless　　d. while

Economic Inequality

Economic inequality is the unequal distribution of income and opportunities between different groups in society. It is a major concern for countries around the world and often people on the bottom rung are trapped in poverty, with little chance to climb up the social ladder. Being born into poverty does not necessarily mean you stay poor, but it is definitely an uphill battle. Education, enhancing skills, and training policies can be used alongside social assistance programs to help people out of poverty and to reduce this damaging inequality.

Economic inequality is usually measured using the distribution of income (the amount of money people are paid) and the distribution of wealth (the amount of wealth people own). This data allows economists to quickly measure and compare the levels of inequality between countries. Aside from comparing inequality between countries, economists also pay attention to the level of inequality between different groups of people within a country.

In 1820, the ratio between the income of the top and bottom twenty percent of the world's population was three to one. By 1991, it was eighty-six to one. This means the rich are truly getting richer. A 2011 study titled "Divided We Stand: Why Inequality Keeps Rising" by the Organization for Economic Co-operation and Development (OECD) sought to explain the causes for this rising inequality by investigating the situation in OECD countries. This study concluded that the following factors have led to increasing inequality:

Changes in the structure of households can play a role. Single-headed households in OECD countries have risen from an average of 15% in the late 1980s to 20% by 2005. This percentage has continued to rise. Assortative mating also seems to contribute to inequality. This refers to the phenomenon of people marrying others with similar backgrounds. This means both partners in a couple are usually from similar socioeconomic backgrounds; so wealthy couples usually stay wealthy. Lastly, working hours have decreased for employees in the bottom wealth percentiles. This is a result of the changing demand for skills. In general, the skills supplied by the lower socioeconomic classes are not as in demand as they used to be.

One major issue facing nations around the world is how to decrease this problematic wealth gap.

Reading Comprehension

Circle the correct words to complete the sentences.

1. Economic inequality is the (equal / unequal) distribution of income and opportunity between different groups in society.
2. Economic inequality is a (concern / concerning) in almost all countries around the world.
3. (Enhance / Enhancing) your skills is one way to get out of poverty.
4. Assortative mating (refers / referring) to the phenomenon of people marrying people of similar backgrounds.
5. Being born into poverty does not automatically mean you stay (poor/ rich).

Questions

1. Why is economic inequality a major problem?
2. How have the structure of households changed around the world?

Free Writing

Do you think your country has a lot of wealth inequality? Explain.

Cultural Spotlight: *Rags-to-Riches Stories*

The expression *rags to riches* refers to any situation in which a person rises from poverty to wealth, and in some cases from absolute obscurity to heights of fame, fortune, and celebrity. This is a common archetype in literature and popular culture as people around the world love to hear these stories and dream about their own shot at money or fame.

One classic story that captures this human desire to see wealth move into the hands of the poor is *Robin Hood*. Robin Hood is a legendary heroic outlaw originally depicted in English folklore and subsequently featured in literature and film. According to legend, he was a highly skilled archer and swordsman. In some versions of the legend, he is depicted as being of noble birth, and in modern retellings he is sometimes depicted as having fought in the Crusades before returning to England to find his lands taken by the Sheriff. Traditionally depicted dressed in Lincoln green, he is said to have robbed from the rich and given to the poor.

Through retellings, additions, and variations, a body of familiar characters associated with Robin Hood has been created. These include his lover, Maid Marian, his band of outlaws, the Merry Men, and his chief opponent, the Sheriff of Nottingham. The Sheriff is often depicted as assisting Prince John in usurping the rightful but absent King Richard, to whom Robin Hood remains loyal. His partisanship of the common people and his hostility to the Sheriff of Nottingham are early recorded features of the legend, but his interest in the rightfulness of the king is not, and neither is his setting in the reign of Richard I. He became a popular folk figure in the Late Middle Ages, and the earliest known ballads featuring him are from the 15th century (1400s).

There have been numerous variations and adaptations of the story over the subsequent years, and the story continues to be widely represented in literature, film, and television. Robin Hood is considered one of the best known tales of English folklore.

The historicity of Robin Hood is not proven and has been debated for centuries. There are numerous references to historical figures with similar names that have been proposed as possible evidence of his existence, some dating back to the late 13th century. At least eight plausible origins to the story have been mooted by historians and folklorists, including suggestions that "Robin Hood" was a stock alias used by or in reference to bandits.

Sentence Structure: ***Make sentences using the examples below.***

1. associated with

   ex) A body of characters associated with Robin Hood has been created.

   ____

2. over the subsequent years

   ex) There have been numerous variations of the story over the subsequent years.

   ____

3. be considered ~

   ex) Robin Hood is considered one of the best known tales of English folklore.

   ____

4. references to ~

   ex) The book is full of references to historical figures.

   ____

5. in reference to ~

   ex) I am calling in reference to next Monday's meeting.

   ____

6. best known ~

   ex) Robin Hood is considered one of the best known tales of English folklore.

   ____

Cultural Spotlight: Music

Listen and circle the correct words. (1)

I Do It For You (Bryan Adams)

Look into my eyes
You will see
What you mean to me
Search your heart
Search your soul
And when you find me there
You'll (search / such) no more

Don't tell me it's not worth tryin' for
You can't tell me it's not worth dyin' for
You know it's true
Everything I do
I do it for you

Look into your heart
You will find
There's nothin' there to (high / hide)
Take me as I am
Take my life
I would give it all
I would sacrifice

Don't tell me it's not worth fightin' for
I can't help it, there's nothin' I want more
You know it's true
Everything I do
I do it for you

There's no love
Like your love
And no other
Could give more love
There's nowhere
Unless you're there
All the time
All the way, yeah

Look into your heart, baby

Oh, you can't tell me it's not worth tryin' for
I can't help it, there's nothin' I want more
Yeah, I would fight for you
I'd (lay / lie) for you
Walk the wire for you
Yeah, I'd (die / dye) for you

You know it's true
Everything I do
Oh I do it for you

Everything I do, darling
And we'll see it through
Oh, we'll see it through
Oh yeah

Yeah search your heart
Search your soul
You can't tell me it ain't worth dying for
Oh yeah I'll be there, yeah
I'd walk the wire for you
I will die for you

Oh yeah I would die for you

I'm going all the way, all the way, yeah

Listen and circle the correct words. (2)

A Time For Us (Andy Williams)

A time for us, someday there'll be
When chains are (ton / torn) by courage born of a love that's free
A time when dreams, so long denied
Can flourish as we (veil / unveil) the love we now must hide

A time for us (last / at last) to see
A life worthwhile for you and me

And with our love through tears and thorns
We will endure as we pass surely through every storm
A time for us, someday there'll be
A new world, a world of shining hope for you and me

A time for us (last / at last) to see
A life worthwhile for you and me

And with our love through tears and thorns
We will endure as we pass surely through every storm
A time for us, someday there'll be
A new world, a world of shining hope for you and me

Listen and fill in the blanks. (1)

I Do It For You (Bryan Adams)

Look into my eyes
You will see
What you mean to me
Search your heart
Search your soul
And when you find me there
You'll search no more

Don't tell me it's not
(   )
You can't tell me it's not
(   )
You know it's true
Everything I do
I do it for you

Look into your heart
You will find
There's nothin' there
(   )
Take me as I am
Take my life
I would give it all
I would sacrifice

Don't tell me it's not worth fightin' for
I can't help it, there's nothin' I want more
You know it's true
Everything I do
I do it for you

There's no love
Like your love
And no other
Could give more love
There's nowhere
(   ) you're there
All the time
All the way, yeah

Look into your heart, baby

Oh, you can't tell me it's not worth tryin' for
I can't help it, there's nothin' I want more
Yeah, I would fight for you
I'd (   ) you
Walk the wire for you
Yeah, I'd die for you

You know it's true
Everything I do
Oh I do it for you

Everything I do, darling
And we'll see it through
Oh, we'll see it through
Oh yeah

Yeah (   )
Search your soul
You can't tell me it ain't worth dying for
Oh yeah I'll be there, yeah
I'd walk the wire for you
I will die for you

Oh yeah I would die for you

I'm going all the way, all the way, yeah

Listen and fill in the blanks. (2)

A Time For Us (Andy Williams)

A time for us, someday there'll be
When (   ) by courage born of a love that's free
A time when dreams, so long denied
Can flourish (   ) the love we now must hide

A time for us at last to see
A life worthwhile for you and me

And with our love through (   )
We will endure as we pass surely through every storm
A time for us, someday there'll be
A new world, a world of shining hope for you and me

A time for us at last to see
A life worthwhile for you and me

And with our love through tears and thorns
We will endure as we (   ) through every storm
A time for us, someday there'll be
A new world, a world of shining hope for you and me

Wrap-Up

Share your opinions:

1. How do you think household structures will change in the future?

2. Do you think wealth inequality is worse in urban or rural areas?

3. Do you think wealth inequality will get worse in the next 50 years?

4. Why is it difficult to get out of poverty?

5. Can you think of any rags-to-riches stories from your country?

Rags-to-Riches Stories

Pros	Cons

UNIT 2
Discrimination

TOPICS

- Racism
- Stereotypes

ICEBREAKERS

- Have you ever heard any stereotypes about other cultures?
- Have you ever experienced discrimination?

Vocabulary Preview

A. *Matching*

1. unjustified (adj.) _____	a. deprive someone of freedom or action
2. restrict (v.) _____	b. rouse from sleep
3. stem (v.) _____	c. not shown to be right or reasonable
4. catastrophe (n.) _____	d. property that is or may be inherited
5. awaken (v.) _____	e. a category of artistic composition
6. backbreaking (adj.) _____	f. an event causing great and often sudden damage or suffering
7. heritage (n.) _____	g. physically demanding
8. genre (n.) _____	h. originate in or be caused by

B. *Fill in the blanks using the vocabulary words above.*

1. Most of his problems _______________ from his drinking.
2. They endured hours of _______________ work.
3. You have made several _______________ claims.
4. Rock was his favorite _______________ of music.
5. Elderly people usually _______________ early in the morning.
6. She was told to _______________ the amount of salt she uses.
7. Folk songs are part of our common _______________.
8. The oil spill was an environmental _______________.

Language Focus (Infinitives and Gerunds)

Choose the best option to complete the following sentences.

1. Discrimination _______ as the unjust or prejudicial treatment of different categories of people.

   a. defines　　b. to define
   c. is defined　　d. defining

2. The students _______ this course will find the correct answers.

   a. to take　　b. taking
   c. took　　d. taken

3. I don't have enough money _______ some furniture for my new house.

   a. buy　　b. to buy
   c. buying　　d. to be bought

4. We are now considering _______ a better maintenance system to increase productivity.

   a. to develop　　b. develop
   c. developed　　d. developing

5. You should stop _______ for your health.

   a. to smoke　　b. smoking
   c. smoke　　d. being smoke

6. The company is having difficulty _______ his placement.

   a. to choose　　b. choose
   c. chose　　d. choosing

7. My husband forgot _______ an email to his colleague, so he is doing it now.

   a. send　　b. sent
   c. to send　　d. sending

Discrimination

Discrimination is the act of making unjustified distinctions between human beings based on the groups, classes, or other categories to which they are perceived to belong. People may be discriminated against on the basis of race, gender, age or sexual orientation, as well as other categories. Discrimination especially occurs when individuals or groups are unfairly treated in a way which is worse than other people are treated, on the basis of their membership in certain groups.

Stereotypes often lead to discrimination. A stereotype is a widely held but fixed and oversimplified image or idea of a particular type of person or thing. Some common gender stereotypes are that *women love to cook or women love to go shopping*. Stereotypes can seem harmless at first, but they often lead to bigger problems like prejudice and discrimination. Think of discrimination as adding actions to prejudices and stereotypes.

Discrimination involves restricting members of one group from opportunities or privileges that are available to members of another group. This unfairness can stem from a wide range of categories, but some of the most common ones are race, gender, and age. Imagine you're applying for a job and you don't get it simply because of the way you look or how old you are. These are clear examples of discrimination.

Throughout history, discrimination has caused a lot of pain and suffering for various groups of people and sadly, it is still a major problem around the world today. Discrimination and racism have even led to terrible tragedies like genocides and slavery. Despite these catastrophes, one incredible thing about the human spirit is our ability to create beautiful art out of hardships and heartaches.

For many people, difficult situations awaken creativity and have led to some incredible music. Two clear examples are the blues and jazz music that were born out of racism in the United States.

The blues is a style of music that began on slave plantations and has deep roots in African-American communities. While doing backbreaking work in cotton fields, many slaves used "field hollers" to get through their miserable days. Many believe these working songs turned into what we know as the blues today. This history is evident as many blues musicians clearly refer to suffering and hardship in their songs. Jazz music stemmed from early blues and has a similar history. Many people love both styles of music not only for the incredible artistry, but also the rich story and heritage of both of these genres.

Reading Comprehension

Circle the correct words to complete the sentences.

1. People may be (discriminated / discrimination) against on the basis of race or gender.
2. Discrimination occurs when individuals or groups are unfairly (treated / treating) in a way which is worse than other people are treated.
3. Discrimination involves (restriction / restricting) members of one group from opportunities or privileges that are available to members of another group.
4. Discrimination and unfairness can (stem / stemming) from a wide range of categories.
5. Difficult situations (awake / awaken) creativity and have led to some incredible music.

Questions

1. What causes discrimination?

2. How did the blues start as a style of music?

Free Writing

Why do you think discrimination has led to some incredible music in the past?

____

____

____

____

____

____

Cultural Spotlight: *Singing through the Pain*

As noted in this unit's reading, discrimination and racism have led to some incredible music. One great example of pain and suffering leading to extraordinary artwork is the song *Strange Fruit* by Billie Holiday. This is a song recorded by Billie Holiday in 1939 that protests the lynching of Black Americans, with lyrics that compare the victims to the fruit of trees. Such lynchings had reached a peak in the Southern United States at the turn of the 20th century, and the great majority of victims were black. The song has been called "a declaration of war" and "the beginning of the civil rights movement."

It was named the song of the century by Time magazine in 1999, and the story of Strange Fruit's conception has entered legend. Originally a poem called Bitter Fruit, it was written by the Jewish school teacher Abel Meeropol under the pseudonym Lewis Allen in response to lynching in US southern states. "I wrote Strange Fruit because I hate lynching, and I hate injustice, and I hate the people who perpetuate it," Meeropol said in 1971. He never witnessed a lynching but it is suggested he wrote Strange Fruit after seeing distressing photographs of a lynching in Indiana. Lynching had begun to subside by the time the poem was published - but photographs seared graphic images into public consciousness.

What happened on the first night Holiday performed Strange Fruit at Café Society foreshadowed the response it would get when released as a record. "The first time I sang it I thought it was a mistake - there wasn't even a patter of applause when I finished. Then a lone person began to clap nervously. Then suddenly everyone was clapping," said Holiday in her autobiography. To hear Holiday sing of "the sudden smell of burning flesh" minutes after her jazz ballads was disquieting. Meeropol wrote: "She gave a startling, most dramatic and effective interpretation, which could jolt an audience out of its complacency anywhere."

As the song became a feature of her sets, Holiday witnessed a range of reactions, from tears to walkouts and racist hecklers. Radio stations in the US and abroad blacklisted it and Holiday's label, Columbia Records, refused to record it. When she toured the song, some proprietors tried discouraging her from singing it for fear of alienating or angering their patrons.

Sentence Structure: ***Make sentences using the examples below.***

1. compare ~ to ~

   ex) The lyrics compare the victims to the fruit of trees.

   ____

2. in response to ~

   ex) It was written by the Jewish school teacher Abel Meeropol in response to lynching.

   ____

3. by the time ~

   ex) Lynching had begun to subside by the time the poem was published.

   ____

4. refuse to ~

   ex) Columbia Records refused to record it.

   ____

5. discourage ~ from ~

   ex) Some proprietors tried discouraging her from singing it.

   ____

Cultural Spotlight: Music

Listen and circle the correct words. (1)

Strange Fruit (Billie Holiday)

(Southern / Sudden) trees bear strange fruit
Blood on the leaves and blood at the (route / root)
Black body swinging in the southern (breeze / breed)
Strange fruit hanging from the poplar trees.
Pastoral scene of the gallant South
The bulging eyes and the twisted mouth
(Sent / Scent) of magnolia, sweet and fresh
Then the (southern / sudden) smell of burning (fresh / flesh)!
Here is fruit for the crows to (flock / pluck)
for the rain to gather,
for the wind to suck
for the sun to rot,
for the trees to drop
Here is a strange and (beat / bitter) crop.

Listen and circle the correct words. (2)

Why I Sing the Blues (B.B. King)

Everybody wants to know
Why I sing the blues
Yes, I say everybody wanna know
Why I sing the blues
Well, I've been around a long time
I really have paid my (dos / dues)
When I first got the blues
They brought me over on a (ship / sheep)
Men were standing over me
And a lot more with a whip
And everybody wanna know
Why I sing the blues
Well, I've been around a long time
Mm, I've really paid my dues
I've laid in a ghetto flat
Cold and (crumb / numb)
I heard the rats tell the bedbugs
To give the roaches some
Everybody wanna know
Why I'm singing the blues
Yes, I've been around a long time
People, I've paid my dues
I (stood / stand) in line
Down at the County Hall
I heard a man say, "We're gonna build
Some new apartments for y'all"
And everybody wanna know
Yes, they wanna know
Why I'm singing the blues
Yes, I've been around a long, long time
Yes, I've really, really paid my dues
Now I'm gonna play Lucille
My kid's gonna grow up
Gonna grow up to be a (tool / fool)
'Cause they ain't got no more room
No more room for him in school
And everybody wanna know
Everybody wanna know
Why I'm singing the blues
I say I've been around a long time
Yes, I've really paid some dues

Listen and fill in the blanks. (1)

Strange Fruit (Billie Holiday)

(   ) trees bear strange fruit

Blood on the leaves and blood (   )

Black body swinging in the (   )

Strange fruit hanging from the poplar trees.

Pastoral scene of the gallant South

The bulging eyes and the twisted mouth

(   ) magnolia, sweet and fresh

Then the (   ) of burning
(   )!

Here is fruit for the (   ) to
(   )

for the rain to gather,

for the wind to suck

for the sun (   ),

for the trees to drop

Here is a strange and (   ) crop.

Listen and fill in the blanks. (2)

Why I Sing the Blues (B.B. King)

Everybody wants to know
Why I sing the blues
Yes, I say everybody wanna know
Why I sing the blues
Well, I've been around a long time
I really (   )
When I first got the blues
They brought me over on a ship
Men were standing over me
And a lot more (   )
And everybody wanna know
Why I sing the blues
Well, I've been around a long time
Mm, I've really paid my dues
I've laid in a ghetto flat
Cold and numb
I heard the rats tell the bedbugs
To give the roaches some
Everybody wanna know
Why I'm singing the blues
Yes, I've been around a long time

People, I've paid my dues
I stood (   )
Down at the County Hall
I heard a man say, "We're gonna build
Some new apartments for y'all"
And everybody wanna know
Yes, they wanna know
Why I'm singing the blues
Yes, I've been around a long, long time
Yes, I've really, really paid my dues
Now I'm gonna play Lucille
My kid's gonna grow up
Gonna grow up to be a fool
'Cause they ain't got no more room
No more (   ) him in school
And everybody wanna know
Everybody wanna know
Why I'm singing the blues
I say I've been around a long time
Yes, I've really paid some dues

Wrap-Up

Share your opinions:

1. Have you ever witnessed age discrimination? Explain.

2. Do you think young children should learn about discrimination?

3. Do you think discrimination is getting worse these days?

4. Do you think discrimination is worse in rural or urban areas?

5. How can we prevent discrimination?

Jazz Music

Pros	Cons

UNIT 3
Child Abuse

TOPICS
- Mental Health
- Physical Abuse

ICEBREAKERS
- Do you think child abuse is a big problem nowadays?
- What are some effective methods to prevent child abuse?

Vocabulary Preview

A. *Matching*

1. intentional (adj.) _____
2. dignity (n.) _____
3. interpersonal (adj.) _____
4. distress (n.) _____
5. abusive (adj.) _____
6. neglect (n.) _____
7. shelter (n.) _____
8. mitigate (v.) _____

a. extreme anxiety, sorrow, or pain
b. relating to relationships between people
c. the state of being uncared for
d. a place giving temporary protection from bad weather or danger
e. done on purpose
f. the state or quality of being worthy of honor or respect
g. make less severe
h. extremely offensive and insulting

B. *Fill in the blanks using the vocabulary words above.*

1. His behavior caused great ________________ for his parents.
2. The successful applicant will have strong ________________ skills.
3. Luckily, she was able to break away from their ________________ relationship.
4. They opened a ________________ to provide temporary housing for homeless people.
5. The law distinguishes between accidental and ________________ crimes.
6. It is unclear how to ________________ the effects of tourism on the island.
7. They were humiliated and lost their sense of ________________.
8. The children suffered from cruelty and ________________.

Language Focus (Participles)

Choose the best option to complete the following sentences.

1. Physically abused children are at risk for later interpersonal problems ______ aggressive behavior.
   a. involved　　b. involve
   c. to be involved　　d. involving

2. The ______ merger will facilitate the ongoing management shift.
   a. planning　　b. plan
   c. plans　　d. planned

3. Everyone knows that Ms. Lee is a hard- ______ person.
   a. working　　b. worked
   c. work　　d. being working

4. We will have to travel over 16 hours to get there, but we will be able to leave on time tomorrow, weather ______.
   a. permit　　b. permitting
   c. permitted　　d. to permit

5. ______ the outcome of the negotiations, the company has no choice but to wait and see.
   a. Considered　　b. Considering
   c. Consider　　d. Consideration

6. Demand for low-tier smartphones remained strong in ______ countries.
   a. emerge　　b. emergion
   c. emerging　　d. emerged

7. I am ______ about my future.
   a. deeply worrying　　b. deep worrying
   c. deep worried　　d. deeply worried

Child Abuse

The WHO defines physical abuse as "Intentional use of physical force against a child that results in harm for the child's health, survival, development or dignity." This includes hitting, beating, shaking and other physical actions. A lot of physical violence against children in the home is inflicted for the purpose of punishment.

Physically abused children are at risk for interpersonal problems later in life. In addition, symptoms of depression and emotional distress are also common features of people who have been physically abused. As many as one-third of children who experience physical abuse are also at risk to become abusive as adults.

Child neglect is the failure of a parent or other person with responsibility for the child, to provide needed food, clothing, shelter, medical care, or supervision to the degree that the child's health, safety or well-being may be threatened with harm.

Many children who have been abused in any form develop some sort of psychological problem. These problems may include: anxiety, depression, eating disorders, codependency, or even a lack of human connections. There is also a slight tendency for children who have been abused to become child abusers themselves.

In the U.S. in 2013, of the 294,000 reported child abuse cases, only 81,124 received any sort of counseling or therapy. Treatment is greatly important for abused children. Meeting weekly with a therapist is a common example of counseling for an abused child. This type of counseling has the potential to greatly improve a young person's mental health, making them more equipped to cope with their difficulties. Additionally, many children are prescribed antidepressant medication to lift their spirits in the wake of abuse. Opinions are mixed on this form of treatment as it can provide some benefits, but it can also lead to dependency.

There are some children who are abused as children without receiving any help or therapy, but they manage to do unexpectedly well later in life despite this upbringing. These children have been termed *dandelion children*, as inspired from the way that dandelions seem to prosper irrespective of soil, sun, drought, or rain. Such children are of high interest in finding factors that mitigate the effects of child abuse.

Reading Comprehension

Circle the correct words to complete the sentences.

1. Physical abuse is (defining / defined) as the intentional use of physical force against a child.
2. (Physical / Physically) abused children are at risk for problems later in life.
3. Depression and emotional distress are also (common / rare) features of people who have been physically abused.
4. Physically abused children are also at risk to become (abusive / abusing) as adults.
5. Federal programs can help to mitigate the (affects / effects) of child abuse.

Questions

1. What are some common features of children who have been abused?

2. What are dandelion children?

Free Writing

What other problems does child abuse cause for a country?

Cultural Spotlight: *Dandelion Children*

Dr. Thomas Boyce has treated children who seem to be completely unfazed by their surroundings as well as those who are extremely sensitive to their environments. Over the years, he began to liken these two types of children to two very different flowers: dandelions and orchids. *Dandelion children* are resilient and able to cope with stress and adversity in their lives while *orchid children* are more sensitive and biologically reactive to their circumstances. Dandelion children often grow up to do incredible things despite their challenging circumstances. One perfect example of a grown up dandelion child is Oprah Winfrey. Oprah went through a lot of adversity in her life but still managed to become incredibly successful.

She is an American media executive, actress, talk show host, television producer, and philanthropist. She is best known for her talk show, The Oprah Winfrey Show, which was the highest-rated television program of its kind in history. She was the richest African American of the 20th century and North America's first black billionaire. She has also been ranked as one of the greatest philanthropists in American history. By 2007, she was sometimes ranked as the most influential woman in the world.

Winfrey was born into poverty in rural Mississippi to a teenage single mother and was later raised in Milwaukee. She has stated that she was molested during her childhood and early teens and became pregnant at 14; her son was born prematurely and died in infancy. Winfrey was then sent to live with the man she calls her father, Vernon Winfrey, a barber in Tennessee, and landed a job in radio while still in high school. By 19, she was a co-anchor for the local evening news. After boosting a third-rate local Chicago talk show to first place, she launched her own production company.

TV columnist Howard Rosenberg said, "She's a roundhouse, a full course meal, big, brassy, loud, aggressive, hyper, laughable, lovable, soulful, tender, low-down, earthy, and hungry. And she may know the way to Phil Donahue's jugular." *Newsday's* Les Payne observed, "Oprah Winfrey is sharper than Donahue, wittier, more genuine, and far better attuned to her audience, if not the world." Martha Bayles of *The Wall Street Journal* wrote, "It's a relief to see a gab-monger with a fond but realistic assessment of her own cultural and religious roots."

Oprah's story is truly inspiring and is a constant reminder for many around the world that you can still be incredibly successful despite growing up in a difficult situation.

Sentence Structure: ***Make sentences using the examples below.***

1. be known for ~

   ex) She is best known for her talk show.

   ____

2. be born into ~

   ex) Winfrey was born into poverty in rural Mississippi

   ____

3. be raised in ~

   ex) She was raised in Milwaukee.

   ____

4. far better

   ex) She is far better attuned to her audience.

   ____

5. a constant reminder

   ex) She is a constant reminder for many around the world that you can still be successful despite growing up in a difficult situation.

   ____

6. was sent to

   ex) Winfrey was then sent to live with the man she calls her father.

   ____

Cultural Spotlight: Music

Listen and circle the correct words. (1)

Luka (Suzanne Vega)

My name is Luka
I (leave / live) on the second floor
I live upstairs from you
Yes I think you've (see / seen) me before
If you (here / hear) something late at night
Some kind of trouble, some kind of fight
Just don't ask me what it was
Just don't ask me what it was
Just don't ask me what it was
I think it's because I'm clumsy
I try not to talk (to / too) loud
Maybe it's because I'm crazy
I try not to act (to, too) proud
They only (heat / hit) until you cry
After that you don't ask why
You just don't argue anymore
You just don't argue anymore
You just don't argue anymore
Yes, I think I'm okay
I (worked / walked) into the door again
If you ask that's what I'll say
And it's not your business anyway
I guess I'd like to be alone
With nothing broken, nothing (throw / thrown)
Just don't ask me how I am
Just don't ask me how I am
Just don't ask me how I am

Listen and circle the correct words. (2)

All You Need Is Love (The Beatles)

Love, love, love
Love, love, love
Love, love, love
There's nothing you can do that can't be done
Nothing you can sing that can't be (song / sung)
Nothing you can say, but you can learn how to play the game
It's easy
Nothing you can make that can't be made
No one you can save that can't be saved
Nothing you can do, but you can learn how to be you in time
It's easy
All you need is love
All you need is love
All you need is love, love
Love is all you need
All you need is love
All you need is love
All you need is love, love
Love is all you need

There's nothing you can know that isn't known
Nothing you can see that isn't shown
There's nowhere you can be that isn't where you're (mend / meant) to be
It's easy
All you need is love
All you need is love
All you need is love, love
Love is all you need
All you need is love (all together now)
All you need is love (everybody)
All you need is love, love
Love is all you need
Yesterday
(Love is all you need)
Oh
Love is all you need
Love is all you need
Oh yeah
Love is all you need
(She loves you, yeah, yeah, yeah)
(She loves you, yeah, yeah, yeah)
(Love is all you need)
(Love is all you need)

Listen and fill in the blanks. (1)

Luka (Suzanne Vega)

My name is Luka
( ) on the second floor
I live upstairs from you
Yes I think ( ) me before
If you hear something late at night
Some kind of trouble, some kind of fight
Just don't ask me what it was
Just don't ask me what it was
Just don't ask me what it was
I think it's because I'm clumsy
I try not to talk ( )
Maybe it's because I'm crazy
I try not to act ( )
They only (heat, hit) until you cry
After that you don't ask why
You just don't argue anymore
You just don't argue anymore
You just don't argue anymore
Yes, I think I'm okay
I ( ) into the door again
If you ask that's what I'll say
And it's not your business anyway
I guess I'd like to be alone
With nothing broken, ( )
Just don't ask me how I am
Just don't ask me how I am
Just don't ask me how I am

Listen and fill in the blanks. (2)

All You Need Is Love (The Beatles)

Love, love, love
Love, love, love
Love, love, love
There's nothing you can do that can't
(   )
Nothing you can sing that can't
(   )
Nothing you can say, but you can learn how to play the game
It's easy
Nothing you can make that can't be made
No one you can save that
(   )
Nothing you can do, but you can learn how to be you in time
It's easy
All you need is love
All you need is love
All you need is love, love
Love is all you need
All you need is love
All you need is love
All you need is love, love
Love is all you need

There's nothing you can know that isn't known
Nothing you can see that isn't shown
There's nowhere you can be that isn't where (   )
It's easy
All you need is love
All you need is love
All you need is love, love
Love is all you need
All you need is love (all together now)
All you need is love (everybody)
All you need is love, love
Love is all you need
Yesterday
(Love is all you need)
Oh
Love is all you need
Love is all you need
Oh yeah
Love is all you need
(She loves you, yeah, yeah, yeah)
(She loves you, yeah, yeah, yeah)
(Love is all you need)
(Love is all you need)

Wrap-Up

Share your opinions:

1. What are some ways to improve mental health?

2. What are some ways to prevent child abuse?

3. Do you think child abuse is more common in urban or rural areas?

4. How can we volunteer to help children in need?

5. Can you think of any famous dandelion children?

Antidepressant Medication

Pros	Cons

UNIT 4

Animal Cruelty

TOPICS

- Factory Farming
- Veganism

ICEBREAKERS

- Do you think exotic animals should be allowed to be kept as pets?
- Do you think animals should be used for commercial research?

Vocabulary Preview

A. *Matching*

1. omission (n.) _____
2. encompass (v.) _____
3. inherently (adv.) _____
4. minimize (v.) _____
5. humane (adj.) _____
6. cramped (adj.) _____
7. husbandry (n.) _____
8. sustainable (adj.) _____

a. having or showing compassion
b. able to be maintained at a certain rate or level
c. in a permanent, essential, or characteristic way
d. a person or thing that has been left out
e. surround and have or hold within
f. the care and breeding of crops and animals
g. reduce to the smallest possible amount or degree
h. feeling or causing someone to feel uncomfortably confined by a lack of space

B. *Fill in the blanks using the vocabulary words above.*

1. The government should do more to promote ________________ farming.
2. Her ________________ from the team was surprising.
3. It is my nature to be kind, gentle, and ________________.
4. They built a moat to ________________ the castle.
5. The company will work to ________________ costs.
6. The kitchen was small and ________________.
7. Firefighting is an ________________ dangerous occupation.
8. The ________________ of domesticated animals should ensure that their needs are fulfilled.

Language Focus (Conditionals)

Choose the best words to complete the following sentences.

1. If I _______ lots of money, I could buy a new car.
   a. have had b. had had
   c. have d. had

2. If I _______ you, I would stay away from her.
   a. was b. am
   c. were d. have been

3. If I _______ harder, my company would not have had to file for bankruptcy.
   a. work b. had worked
   c. did work d. had work

4. If Park _______ Kim, such a meeting would have been significant in itself.
   a. have met b. had met
   c. has met d. had been met

5. I really wish that I _______ she was going to be absent today so that I could have avoided coming in so early.
   a. known b. know
   c. had knew d. had known

6. As was mentioned in our earlier announcement, the plane cannot depart _______ all passengers are seated with their seatbelts fastened.
   a. if b. when
   c. unless d. but

7. _______ you need secretarial services during your stay, please contact the hotel receptionist.
   a. May b. Whether
   c. Perhaps d. Should

Animal Cruelty

Cruelty to animals, also called animal abuse, animal neglect or animal cruelty, is the infliction by omission (neglect) or by commission by humans of suffering or harm upon any non-human. More narrowly, it can be the causing of harm or suffering for specific achievement, such as killing animals for entertainment. Cruelty to animals sometimes encompasses inflicting harm or suffering as an end in itself.

Some think that the animal welfare position holds that there is nothing inherently wrong with using animals for human purposes, such as food, clothing, entertainment, fun and research, but that it should be done in a way that minimizes unnecessary pain and suffering, sometimes referred to as "humane" treatment. Others have argued that the definition of 'unnecessary' varies widely and could include virtually all current use of animals.

One current issue in the fight for animal rights is the use of puppy mills. A puppy mill, also known as a puppy farm, is a commercial dog breeding facility characterized by quick breeding and poor conditions. These puppies are sold by the owner of the mill for profit. Due to the frequently poor breeding conditions in puppy mills, puppies bred there often suffer from health and social problems. Puppies raised in a cramped environment shared by many other dogs become poorly socialized to other dogs and to humans. Dogs are then transported over long distances in poor conditions, sometimes resulting in animal stress and death.

Another important issue is factory farming. Factory farming is a type of intensive agriculture, specifically an approach to animal husbandry designed to maximize production, while minimizing costs. To achieve this, agribusinesses keep livestock such as cattle, poultry, and fish at high stocking densities, at large scale, and using modern machinery, biotechnology, and global trade. The main products of this industry are meat, milk and eggs for human consumption. There are issues regarding whether intensive animal farming is sustainable or ethical. There is a continuing debate over the benefits, risks and ethics of intensive animal farming. The issues include the efficiency of food production; animal welfare; health risks and the environmental impact.

With these issues in mind, it is clear that we need to find a better way to peacefully coexist with the animals of the world.

Reading Comprehension

Circle the correct words to complete the sentences.

1. Factory farming is a clear example of (cruel / cruelty) to animals.
2. Cruelty sometimes (encompasses / encompassing) inflicting harm on others.
3. Some puppies are raised in (cramped / cramping) environments.
4. Animals are sometimes transported (over / under) long distances in poor conditions.
5. There is a (continue / continuing) debate over the benefits and risks of animal farming.

Questions

1. What are puppy mills?
2. What is factory farming?

Free Writing

Do you think animal abuse is a large problem nowadays? Explain.

Cultural Spotlight: *The Rise of Veganism*

Why is Demand for Vegan Food Growing? Aside from innovation, another fundamental reason behind the growth of the vegan food market is rising consumer awareness of the health consequences of eating animal products, as well as the ethical and environmental impact of animal agriculture.

According to a recent study, nearly 114 million Americans are intending to eat more vegan food for health reasons. Research has linked the consumption of animal products with serious health conditions, including diabetes, heart disease, and cancer.

It's not only their own health that is motivating consumers to ditch animal products, but the health of the planet too. People are becoming more and more aware of the impact that animal agriculture has on the environment.

A major United Nations report revealed that we do not have many years left to prevent a climate change crisis. Around the same time, the global organization's Environment Programme (UNEP) named tackling meat production and consumption as the "world's most urgent problem."

Awareness is growing around how billions of animals around the world are exploited for human gain. Some popular documentaries like *Dominion* and *Earthlings* have highlighted this massive problem. These films showcase the suffering that animals go through in the meat, dairy, and egg industries, but also show how animals are used for research, fashion, and entertainment.

Celebrities are also getting involved in raising awareness. Actor Joaquin Phoenix narrated both *Dominion* and *Earthlings*, and musician Miley Cyrus continuously speaks out against animal cruelty for food and fashion. A recent campaign by Mercy for Animals highlighted how McDonald's treats its chickens. They're bred to be so large they can barely walk without being in pain and are kept in tiny cramped cages before they are turned into McNuggets.

In 2018, it was revealed that the top reason people ditched meat, dairy, and eggs was for animal welfare-related reasons. In other words, they stopped eating meat in order to protect animals. The results of another famous study showed that nearly half of all meat-eaters would rather turn vegetarian than kill an animal themselves for dinner.

Sentence Structure: ***Make sentences using the examples below.***

1. Aside from ~ another

   ex) Aside from innovation, another fundamental reason behind the growth of the vegan food market is rising consumer awareness of the health consequences of eating animal products.

   ____

2. not only ~ but also

   ex) It's not only their own health that is motivating consumers to ditch animal products, but also the health of the planet.

   ____

3. intending to

   ex) People are intending to eat more vegan food for health reasons.

   ____

4. revealed that

   ex) A major United Nations report revealed that we do not have many years left to prevent a climate change crisis.

   ____

5. named ~ as

   ex) The group named tackling meat production and consumption as the "world's most urgent problem."

   ____

6. to highlight

   ex) Some popular documentaries have highlighted this massive problem.

   ____

Cultural Spotlight: Music

Listen and circle the correct words. (1)

Memory (Barbra Streisand)

Midnight, not a sound from the pavement
Has the moon lost her memory?
She is smiling alone
In the lamplight, the (wither / withered) leaves collect at my feet
And the wind begins to moan

Memory, all alone in the moonlight
I can dream of the old days
Life was beautiful then
I remember the time I knew what happiness was
Let the memory live again

Every street lamp seems to beat
A fatalistic warning
Someone mutters and the street lamp sputters
And soon it will be morning

Daylight, I must wait for the sunrise
I must think of a new life
And I mustn't give in
When (dawn / the dawn) comes, tonight will be a memory too
And a new day will begin

(Burn / Burnt) out ends of smoky days
The stale, cold smell of morning
A street lamp dies, another night is over
Another day is dawning

Touch me, it's so easy to leave me
All alone with the memory
Of my days in the sun
If you touch me, you'll understand what happiness is
Look, a new day has begun

Listen and circle the correct words. (2)

That Doggie in the Window (Patti Page)

How much is that doggie in the window?
The one with the waggly tail
How much is that doggie in the window?
I do hope that doggie's for (sail / sale)

I must take a trip to California
And (live / leave) my poor sweetheart alone
If he has a dog, he won't be lonesome
And the doggie will have a good home

How much is that doggie in the window?
The one with the waggly tail
How much is that doggie in the window?
I do hope that doggie's for (sail / sale)

I read in the papers there are robbers
With flashlights that shine in the dark
My love needs a doggie to protect him
And scare them away with one (bark / dark)

I don't want a bunny···

I don't want a bunny or a kitty
I don't want a parrot that talks
I don't want a bowl of little fishies
He can't take a goldfish for a walk

How much is that doggie in the window?
The one with the waggly tail
How much is that doggie in the window?
I do hope that doggie's for sale

Listen and fill in the blanks. (1)

Memory (Barbra Streisand)

Midnight, not a sound from the pavement
Has the moon lost her memory?
She is smiling alone
In the lamplight, the (   ) collect at my feet
And the wind begins to moan

Memory, all alone in the moonlight
I can dream of the old days
Life was beautiful then
I remember the time I knew what happiness was
Let the memory live again

Every street lamp seems to beat
A fatalistic warning
Someone (   ) and the street lamp sputters
And soon it will be morning

Daylight, I must wait for the sunrise
I must think of a new life
And I mustn't (   )
When the dawn comes, tonight will be a memory too
And a new day will begin

(   ) ends of smoky days
The stale, cold smell of morning
A street lamp dies, another night is over
Another day is dawning

Touch me, it's so easy to leave me
All alone with the memory
Of my days in the sun
If you touch me, you'll understand what happiness is
Look, a new day has begun

Listen and fill in the blanks. (2)

That Doggie in the Window (Patti Page)

How much is that doggie in the window?
The one with the waggly tail
How much is that doggie in the window?
I do hope that doggie's (   )

I must take a trip to California
And (   ) my poor sweetheart alone
If he has a dog, he won't be lonesome
And the doggie will have a good home

How much is that doggie in the window?
The one with the waggly tail
How much is that doggie in the window?
I do hope that doggie's (   )

I read in the papers there are robbers
With flashlights that shine in the dark
My love needs a doggie to protect him
And scare them away with one bark

I don't want a bunny···

I don't want a bunny or a kitty
I don't want a parrot that talks
I don't want a bowl of little fishies
He can't take a goldfish for a walk

How much is that doggie in the window?
The one with the waggly tail
How much is that doggie in the window?
I do hope that doggie's for sale

Wrap-Up

Share your opinions:

1. Do you think factory farming is a big problem? Why?

2. Do you think puppy mills are a big problem? Why?

3. Do you think it is possible to stop factory farming?

4. How can we prevent animal abuse?

5. Have you ever tried vegan food? Did you like it?

Veganism

Pros	Cons

UNIT 5

Bullying

TOPICS

- Cyberbullying
- Herd Mentality

ICEBREAKERS

- Was bullying a problem at your high school?
- Do you think cyberbullying is more dangerous than bullying in person?

Vocabulary Preview

A. *Matching*

1. coercion (n.) _____
2. habitual (adj.) _____
3. imbalance (n.) _____
4. hostile (adj.) _____
5. contemporary (adj.) _____
6. legal (adj.) _____
7. assert (v.) _____
8. rationalization (n.) _____

a. done constantly or as a habit
b. unfriendly, opposed
c. based on or related to the law
d. cause others to recognize one's authority by forceful behavior
e. lack of proportion between corresponding things
f. the action of attempting to explain or justify behavior with reasons, even if these reasons are not appropriate
g. occurring in the present
h. the practice of persuading someone to do something by using threats

B. *Fill in the blanks using the vocabulary words above.*

1. Her depression is caused by a chemical _______________ in the brain.
2. They used _______________ to obtain the confession.
3. Young people tend to prefer _______________ music.
4. The boss was reluctant to _______________ his authority over his employees.
5. No amount of _______________ could justify his actions.
6. There are _______________ consequences for companies breaking the rules.
7. He's a _______________ smoker. He has a cigarette every morning.
8. Their _______________ looks showed that he was unwelcome.

Language Focus (Verbs and Agreement)

Choose the best option to complete the following sentences.

1. The researcher says bullying ______ when a person is "exposed, repeatedly and over time, to negative actions on the part of one or more other persons."
   a. is occurred b. occurring
   c. occurs d. has been occurred

2. Everyone ______ that we are from Korea.
   a. knows b. is knowing
   c. know d. have been known

3. Mathematics ______ one of the most difficult subjects to me.
   a. is b. are
   c. has d. have

4. Every Sunday night I ______ the TV show 'I'm a Singer' on MBC.
   a. watch b. watches
   c. watched d. have watched

5. The project must ______ at once.
   a. is done b. be done
   c. should done d. would be done

6. The talks between defense chiefs of the two countries ______ on Friday.
   a. were held b. was held
   c. were being held d. was being held

7. A large number of people ______ travel overseas during the upcoming holiday.
   a. is expected to b. is expect to
   c. are expected to d. was expected to

Bullying

One hot topic in the world of education is the widespread problem of bullying. Bullying, or peer abuse as it is sometimes called, can happen in any context in which humans interact with each other. Bullying seems to exist in every culture and is defined as the use of force, coercion, or threat, to abuse and assert domination over others.

Bullying is divided into four basic types of abuse: psychological, verbal, physical, and cyber. The behavior is often repeated and habitual. One essential prerequisite is the perception (by the bully or by others) of an imbalance of physical or social power. This imbalance of power distinguishes bullying from conflict.

This hostile action hurts the victim physically, mentally, or emotionally. Rationalizations of such behavior sometimes include differences of social class, race, religion, gender, sexual orientation, appearance, behavior, body language, personality, reputation, lineage, strength, size, or ability.

The main platform for bullying in contemporary culture is on social media websites where pictures and rumors can spread rapidly. This creates new problems when compared to the verbal and physical bullying of past generations. Students nowadays experience more anxiety partly because of the prevalence of cyberbullying and social media.

Andrew Smythe, the managing director of *BeatBullying* notes that "Cyberbullying has changed the landscape. Before, bullying was something that you could address at the school level, now it requires different organisations - local authorities, the police and social services - to collaborate." This need for all members of a community to collaborate can be difficult to organize and overwhelming for teachers when it is not set up properly.

Different cultures define and respond to bullying in different ways. Some countries have no legal definition of bullying while others have very specific definitions and guidelines. Finland has a successful anti-bullying campaign called KiVa. This program focuses on teaching bystanders what to do if they see bullying through computer games and simulations. Other countries like Korea use comprehensive prevention education and role plays to prevent bullying in schools.

As time marches on, one major challenge will be figuring out the best methods of preventing cyberbullying in schools.

Reading Comprehension

Circle the correct words to complete the sentences.

1. Bullying is the use of force to (abusing / abuse) others.
2. Bullying is characterized by hostile intent and a(n) (balance / imbalance) of power.
3. Bullying can also be called peer (support / abuse).
4. A bullying culture can develop in (a specific / any) context in which humans interact.
5. Bullying is (divided / dividing) into four basic types of abuse.

Questions

1. What are the four types of bullying?

2. Which type of bullying do you think is the most harmful?

Free Writing

How can schools prevent bullying? Share some ideas below.

Cultural Spotlight: *Herd Mentality*

Herd mentality describes how people can be influenced by their peers to adopt certain behaviors on a largely emotional, rather than rational, basis. When individuals are affected by herd mentality, they may make different decisions than they would have individually. This mentality is common for teenagers and often leads to peer pressure and bullying. At times, this can even lead to gang violence.

Dangerous Minds is a famous movie that deals with gang mentality and violence in a school setting. In this movie, LouAnne Johnson, a discharged U.S. Marine, applies for a teaching job in high school, and is surprised and pleased to be offered the position immediately. Showing up the next day to begin teaching, however, she finds herself confronted with a classroom of tough, sullen teenagers, all from low income working-class backgrounds, involved in gang warfare and drug pushing, flatly refusing to engage with anything.

They immediately coin the nickname "White Bread" for LouAnne, due to her race and apparent lack of authority, to which LouAnne responds by returning the next day in a leather jacket and teaching them karate. The students show some interest in such activities, but are uninterested when LouAnne tries to teach the curriculum.

Desperate to reach the students, LouAnne devises classroom exercises that teach similar principles to the prescribed work, but using themes and language that appeal to the students. She also tries to motivate them by giving them all an A grade from the beginning of the year, and arguing that the only thing required of them is that they maintain it.

In order to introduce them to poetry, LouAnne uses the lyrics of Bob Dylan's "Mr. Tambourine Man" to teach symbolism and metaphor; once this is achieved, she progresses on to Dylan Thomas's "Do not go gentle into that good night." LouAnne rewards the students liberally, using candy bars, reward incentives, and a trip to a theme park. Her methods attract the anger of the school authorities, George Grandey and Carla Nichols, who try to force her to remain within the curriculum.

Particular individual students attract LouAnne's attention for their personal problems. Raul Sanchero is a boy who is frequently involved in gang warfare and street crime. LouAnne tries to encourage him to focus by paying a special visit to his family to congratulate him on his work, and going to dinner with him as a way of instilling confidence and self-respect.

Emilio Ramirez is her most troublesome personal "project" as he believes strongly in a sense of personal honor that prevents him from asking for help. When LouAnne discovers that his life is in danger because of a personal grudge held by a recently released thug, she tries to protect him. She advises him to seek help from Principal Grandey. The next day, Emilio visits Grandey, but Grandey (not realizing that Emilio is in serious danger) instantly dismisses him because he neglected to knock on Grandey's door before entering his office.

Feeling rejected, Emilio leaves the school and is subsequently killed by his enemy. Heartbroken by her failure to protect Emilio and angry at the indifferent school system for contributing to his death, LouAnne announces to the class her intention to leave the school at the end of the academic year. The students immediately break down, begging her not to leave. Overwhelmed by their unbridled display of emotion, she decides to stay.

Sentence Structure: ***Make sentences using the examples below.***

1. apply for ~

   ex) He applied for a teaching job in high school.

   ____

2. be involved in ~

   ex) He is frequently involved in gang warfare

   ____

3. force ~ to

   ex) They try to force her to stay there.

   ____

4. prevent ~ from

   ex) That prevents him from asking for help.

   ____

Cultural Spotlight: Music

Listen and circle the correct words. (1)

Gangsta's Paradise (Coolio)

As I walk through the valley of the shadow of (death / dead)
I take a look at my life and realize there's nothin' left
'Cause I've been blasting and laughing so long,
That even my mama thinks that my mind is gone
But I (ain't / aren't) never crossed a man that didn't deserve it
Me be treated like a punk you know that's unheard of
You better watch how you're talking and where you're walking
Or you and your homies might be lined in chalk
I really hate to trip but I gotta loc
As they croak, I see myself in the pistol smoke, fool
I'm the kinda G the little homies wanna be like
On my knees in the night saying (pray / prayers) in the streetlight

*Been spending most their lives, living in the gangsta's paradise(2)
Keep spending most our lives, living in the gangsta's paradise(2)*
Look at the situation they got me facin'
I can't live a normal life, I was raised by the streets
So I gotta be down with the hood team
Too much television watching got me chasing dreams
I'm an educated fool with money on my mind
Got my 10 in my hand and a gleam in my eye
I'm a loc'd out gangsta set trippin' banger
And my homies is down so don't arouse my anger, fool
Death ain't nothing but a heartbeat away,
I'm living life, do or die, what can I say
I'm 23 now, but will I live to see 24
The way things are going I don't know

Tell me why are we so blind to see
That the ones we hurt are you and me

Been spending most their lives, living in the gangsta's paradise(2)
Keep spending most our lives, living in the gangsta's paradise(2)
Power and the money, money and the power
Minute after minute, hour after hour
Everybody's running, but half of them ain't looking
What's going on in the kitchen, but I don't know what's cookin'
They say I gotta learn, but nobody's here to teach me
If they can't understand it, how can they reach me
I guess they can't, I guess they won't
I guess they front, that's why I know my life is out of luck, fool

Been spending most their lives, living in the gangsta's paradise(2)
Keep spending most our lives, living in the gangsta's paradise(2)
Tell me why are we so blind to see
That the ones we hurt are you and me(2)

Listen and circle the correct words. (2)

To Sir, With Love (Lulu)

Those schoolgirl days of telling (tales / tails) and biting nails are gone
But in my mind I know they will still live on and on
But how do you thank someone who has taken you from crayons to perfume?
It isn't easy, but I'll try

If you wanted the sky I would write across the sky in letters
That would (so / soar) a thousand feet high 'To Sir, With Love'

The time has come for closing books and long last looks must end
And as I leave, I know that I am leaving my best friend
A friend who taught me (light / right) from wrong and weak from strong
That's a lot to learn, but what can I give you in return?

If you wanted the moon I would try to make a start
But I would rather you let me give my heart 'To Sir, With Love'

Listen and fill in the blanks. (1)

Gangsta's Paradise (Coolio)

As I walk through the valley of the
(   )

I take a look at my life and realize there's nothin' left
'Cause I've been blasting and laughing so long,
That even my mama thinks that my mind is gone
But I ain't never crossed a man that didn't deserve it
Me be treated like a punk you know that's unheard of
You better watch how you're talking and where (   )
Or you and your homies might be lined in chalk
I really hate to trip but I gotta loc
As they croak, I see myself in the pistol smoke, fool
I'm the kinda G the little homies wanna be like
On my knees in the night
(   ) in the streetlight

Been spending most their lives, living in the gangsta's paradise(2)
Keep spending most our lives, living in the gangsta's paradise(2)
Look at the situation they got me facin'
I can't live a normal life, I was raised by the streets
So I gotta be down with the hood team
Too much television watching got me chasing dreams
I'm an educated fool with money on my mind
Got my 10 in my hand and a gleam in my eye
I'm a loc'd out gangsta set trippin' banger
And my homies is down so don't
(   ) anger, fool
Death ain't nothing but a heartbeat away,
I'm living life, do or die, what can I say
I'm 23 now, but will I live to see 24
The way things are going I don't know

Tell me why are we so blind to see
That the ones we hurt are you and me

Been spending most their lives, living in the gangsta's paradise(2)
Keep spending most our lives, living in the gangsta's paradise(2)
Power and the money, money and the power
Minute after minute, hour after hour
Everybody's running, but half of them ain't looking
What's going on in the kitchen, but I don't know what's cookin'
They say I gotta learn, but nobody's here to teach me
If they can't understand it, how can they reach me
I guess they can't, I guess they won't
I guess they front, that's why I know my life is (   ), fool

Been spending most their lives, living in the gangsta's paradise(2)
Keep spending most our lives, living in the gangsta's paradise(2)
Tell me why are we so blind to see
That the ones we hurt are you and me(2)

Listen and fill in the blanks. (2)

To Sir, With Love (Lulu)

Those schoolgirl, days of ( ) and
( ) are gone
But in my mind I know they will still live on and on
But how do you thank someone who has taken you from crayons to perfume?
It isn't easy, but I'll try

If you wanted the sky I would write across the sky in letters
That would ( ) feet high 'To Sir, With Love'

The time has come for closing books and long last looks
( )
And as I leave, I know that I am leaving my best friend
A friend who taught me ( ) and weak from strong
That's a lot to learn, but what can I give you in return?

If you wanted the moon I would try to make a start
But I would rather you let me give my heart 'To Sir, With Love'

Wrap-Up

Share your opinions:

1. Do you think bullying is worse in elementary or middle school?

2. Do you think bullying is worse in middle or high school?

3. Is bullying still a problem in university?

4. If you could change one thing about the education system in your country, what would you change? Why?

5. Have you ever witnessed herd mentality?

University Life

Pros	Cons

UNIT 6
Refugees

TOPICS
- Resettlement
- Uplifting Songs

ICEBREAKERS
- Think of two basic human rights. Share them with the class.
- Can you think of any uplifting songs?

Vocabulary Preview

A. *Matching*

1. refugee (n.) ______
2. displace (v.) ______
3. resettlement (n.) ______
4. exploitation (n.) ______
5. integrate (v.) ______
6. workforce (n.) ______
7. traumatic (adj.) ______
8. buffer (v.) ______

a. emotionally disturbing or distressing
b. the action of treating someone unfairly in order to benefit from their work
c. force to leave their home or usual place
d. the people engaged in or available for work
e. a person who has been forced to leave their country in order to escape something
f. lessen or moderate the impact of something
g. the settlement of people in a different place
h. combine one thing with another so that they become a whole

B. *Fill in the blanks using the vocabulary words above.*

1. Migrant workers are vulnerable to ________________ by local businesses.
2. Women now account for almost 50% of the ________________.
3. Many of the ________________ villages are in isolated areas.
4. The natural disaster was a ________________ experience.
5. The war has ________________ many people.
6. The government created an official ________________ program for refugees and displaced people.
7. The trees help ________________ the house from the hot summer sun.
8. The car's design ________________ art and technology.

Language Focus (Active and Passive Voice)

Choose the best option to complete the following sentences.

1. A refugee is a displaced person who ______ to cross national boundaries and who cannot return home safely.
   a. forced b. has forced
   c. has been forced d. is forcing

2. Refugees ______ many barriers in receiving countries in finding and sustaining employment commensurate with their experience and expertise.
   a. encounter b. are encountered
   c. have been encountered d. encountering

3. He ______ the company to agree to the contract terms.
   a. was demanded b. demanded
   c. was urged d. urged

4. Any application form should ______ out completely.
   a. fill b. be filled
   c. to fill d. filling

5. The prosecution ______ issue a summons this week for him.
   a. is expected to b. is expected
   c. is expect to d. expect to

6. In front of the Museum, visitors will see the statue, which ______ in 1999.
   a. will build b. was built
   c. build d. built

7. The Ministry of Education initially ______ the school's merger plan.
   a. was objected to b. was objected
   c. objected to d. object to

Refugees

A refugee, generally speaking, is a displaced person who has been forced to cross national boundaries and who cannot return home safely. Refugees can be displaced because of conflict, violence, human rights violations, persecution, and natural hazards.

Headquartered in Geneva, Switzerland, the Office of the United Nations High Commissioner for Refugees (UNHCR) was established on December 14 in 1950. It protects and supports refugees at the request of a government or the United Nations and assists in providing durable solutions, such as return or resettlement.

Refugee populations consist of people who are terrified and are away from familiar surroundings. There can be instances of exploitation at the hands of enforcement officials, citizens of the host country, and even United Nations peacekeepers. These human rights violations have been documented a number of times.

Integrating refugees into the workforce is one of the most important steps to giving them a chance at a better life. Many refugees are unemployed, under-employed, under-paid and work in the informal economy, if not receiving public assistance. Refugees encounter many barriers in their new countries when looking for jobs and sustaining employment commensurate with their experience and expertise.

Refugee children come from many different backgrounds, and their reasons for resettlement are even more diverse. The number of refugee children has continued to increase as conflicts interrupt communities at a global scale. In

2014 alone, there were approximately 32 armed conflicts in 26 countries around the world, and this period saw the highest number of refugees ever recorded. Refugee children experience traumatic events in their lives that can affect their learning capabilities, even after they have resettled in new countries.

The histories of refugee students are often hidden from educators, resulting in cultural misunderstandings. However, when teachers, school staff, and peers help refugee students develop a positive cultural identity, it can help buffer the negative effects their traumatic experiences have on them. Therefore, it is important to understand the cultural differences between newly arrived refugees and the people in their host country.

Reading Comprehension

Circle the correct words to complete the sentences.

1. A refugee is a (displace / displaced) person.
2. Refugee populations (consist / consisting) of people who are terrified.
3. (Integration / Integrating) refugees into the workforce is a very important step.
4. Refugees encounter (many / few) barriers in their host countries.
5. The histories of refugee students are (often / never) hidden from educators.

Questions

1. What is the UNHCR? What does it do?

2. How can schools help refugee children?

Free Writing

Why do you think it is difficult for refugees to integrate into new countries?

Cultural Spotlight: *Uplifting Songs*

Uplifting music has an incredible ability to raise the human spirit and help us get through hard times, such as the experience of life as a refugee. Musicians have made songs in response to tragedies and suffering for a very long time. One classic example of an uplifting song is *Imagine* by John Lennon.

Imagine is the most successful song from John Lennon's solo career and it has had a massive impact across the globe. *Rolling Stone* described "Imagine" as Lennon's "greatest musical gift to the world," and ranked it at number three on its list of "The 500 Greatest Songs of All Time," describing it as "an enduring hymn of solace and promise that has carried us through extreme grief."

On January 1, 2005, the Canadian Broadcasting Corporation named *Imagine* the greatest song in the past 100 years as voted by listeners. It has been accepted all over the world as a beautiful song of peace and unity. Some of the biggest artists from every generation have covered this song at important concerts since its release. *Imagine* is especially popular at benefit concerts for issues like fighting poverty, world hunger, or the refugee crisis.

The lyrics encourage listeners to imagine a world at peace without the barriers of borders or the divisions of religion and nationality. Lennon also encourages us to consider the possibility that all of humanity could live unattached to material possessions.

However, not everyone liked this song when it first came out. Disguised within the uplifting lyrics are some ideas that challenge society as we know it. Some critics claimed this song promoted communism because it asks the listener to imagine a world without possessions where we all work together. Some governments around the world were incredibly concerned about the spread of communism at this time, so that made this a very controversial song for some.

Additionally, some religious groups even asked Lennon to change one specific line in the song. When Lennon asked us to imagine a world with "no religion," one church group asked him to change that line to "one religion." Lennon always refused and said that would defeat the whole purpose of the song.

Sentence Structure: ***Make sentences using the examples below.***

1. in response to

   ex) Musicians have made songs in response to tragedies and suffering for a very long time.

   ____

2. not everyone

   ex) However, not everyone liked this song when it first came out.

   ____

3. ranked it at

   ex) Rolling Stone ranked it at number three on its list of *The 500 Greatest Songs of All Time.*

   ____

4. accepted ~ as ~

   ex) It has been accepted all over the world as a beautiful song of peace and unity.

   ____

5. ask ~ to ~

   ex) One church group asked him to change that line.

   ____

Cultural Spotlight: Music

Listen and circle the correct words. (1)

Imagine (John Lennon)

Imagine there's no heaven
It's easy if you try
No hell below us
Above us only sky
Imagine all the people
(Leaving / Living) for today... Aha-ah...

Imagine there's no countries
It isn't hard to do
Nothing to kill or (die / dye) for
And no religion, (too / to)
Imagine all the people
Living life in (piece / peace)... You...

You may say I'm a dreamer
But I'm not the only (won / one)
I hope someday you'll join us
And the world will be as one

Imagine no possessions
I wonder if you can
No need for (greed / grid) or hunger
A brotherhood of man
Imagine all the people
Sharing all the world··· You...

You may say I'm a dreamer
But I'm not the only one
I hope someday you'll join us
And the world will live as (won / one)

Listen and circle the correct words. (2)

We Are the World (Various Artists)

There comes a time when we (need / heed) a certain call
when the (word / world) must come together as one
There are people dying
Oh, and it's time to (land / lend) a hand to life
The greatest gift of all
We can't go on pretending day-by-day
That someone, somewhere will soon make a change
We're all a part of God's great big family
And the truth, you know, love is all we need
We are the world We are the children
We are the (one / ones) who make a brighter day, so let's start giving
There's a choice we're making
We're saving our own (life / lives)
It's true we'll make a better day, just you and me
Oh, (sand / send) them your heart
So they know that someone cares
And their lives will be stronger and free
As God has shown us by turning stones to bread
And so we all must (land / lend) a helping hand

When you're down and out, (there / their) seems no hope at all
But if you just believe there's (know / no) way we can fall
Well, well, well, well let us realize
Oh, that a change can only come
When we stand together (us / as) one, yeah, yeah, yeah

Listen and fill in the blanks. (1)

Imagine (John Lennon)

Imagine there's no heaven
It's easy if you try
No hell below us
above us only sky
Imagine all the people
(   ) today... Aha-ah...

Imagine there's no countries
It isn't hard to do
Nothing to kill or (   )
And no religion, (   )
Imagine all the people
Living life (   )... You...

You may say I'm a dreamer
But I'm not (   )
I hope someday you'll join us
And the world will be as one

Imagine no possessions
I wonder if you can
No need (   ) or hunger
A brotherhood of man
Imagine all the people
Sharing all the world... You...

You may say I'm a dreamer
But I'm not the only one
I hope someday you'll join us

And the world will live (   )

Listen and fill in the blanks. (2)

We Are the World (Various Artists)

There comes a time when we (   ) a certain call
when the (   ) must come together as one
There are people dying
Oh, and it's time to (   ) to life
The greatest gift of all
We can't go on pretending day-by-day
That someone, somewhere will soon make a change
We're all a part of God's great big family
And the truth, you know, love is all we need
We are the world   We are the children
We are the ones who make a brighter day, so let's start giving
There's a choice we're making
We're saving our own (   )
It's true we'll make a better day, just you and me
Oh, (   ) them your heart
So they know that someone cares
And their lives will be stronger and free
As God has shown us by turning stones to bread
And so we all must lend a helping hand

When you're down and out, there seems no hope at all
But if you just believe there's no way we can fall
Well, well, well, well let us realize
Oh, that a change can only come
When we stand together (   ), yeah, yeah, yeah

Wrap-Up

Share your opinions:

1. How can we help refugees?
2. What can we learn from refugees?
3. Do you think all countries should accept refugees?
4. Make a list of uplifting songs from your country.
5. What is your favorite uplifting song?

Moving and Resettlement

Pros	Cons

ANSWER KEY

CHAPTER 1

[Unit 1]

Vocab Preview:

A: 1.d 2.g 3.a 4.b 5.h 6.c 7.e 8.f

B: 1. segregate 2. negotiate 3. stimulus 4. integral 5. magnify
6. nonverbal 7. extensive 8. symmetry

Language Focus: 1.b 2.a 3.d 4.d 5.c 6.c 7.d

Reading Comprehension:

1. segregated 2. to communicate 3. to negotiate 4. nonverbal 5. fewer

[Unit 2]

Vocab Preview:

A: 1.e 2.a 3.d 4.b 5.c 6.f 7.h 8.g

B: 1. differentiate 2. adolescent 3. ambiguous 4. vigor 5. guardian
6. construct 7. adulthood 8. mindset

Language Focus: 1.d 2.c 3.d 4.b 5.b 6.c 7.b

Reading Comprehension:

1. experience 2. time of life 3. defines 4. reflects 5. constructing

[Unit 3]

Vocab Preview:

A: 1.b 2.e 3.a 4.h 5.c 6.g 7.f 8.d

B: 1. implemented 2. roughly 3. attire 4. harmonious 5. calm
6. Varies 7. medicinal 8. intricately

Language Focus: 1.b 2.d 3.d 4.a 5.a 6.c 7.b

Reading Comprehension:
1. varies 2. hours 3. medicinal 4. dances 5. newlyweds

[Unit 4]

Vocab Preview:
A: 1.c 2.e 3.a 4.h 5.g 6.d 7.f 8.b
B: 1. boisterous 2. vessel 3. symbolically 4. prototypical 5. cathartic
6. ingrained 7. lavish 8. fuse

Language Focus: 1.a 2.b 3.b 4.a 5.b 6.a 7.d

Reading Comprehension:
1. deeply 2. mourners 3. unique 4. lavish 5. exposes

[Unit 5]

Vocab Preview:
A: 1.b 2.h 3.e 4.f 5.a 6.g 7.c 8.d
B: 1. demographics 2. populous 3. inferior 4. geographical 5. continuous
6. adherent 7. indigenous 8. affiliation

Language Focus: 1.c 2.a 3.a 4.a 5.a 6.b 7.b

Reading Comprehension:
1. identifies 2. demographic 3. form 4. most 5. discrimination

[Unit 6]

Vocab Preview:
A: 1.e 2.h 3.a 4.g 5.c 6.d 7.b 8.f

B: 1. restriction 2. beard 3. corrupt 4. pacifism 5. dominant
6. imply 7. espouse 8. unconventional

Language Focus: 1.b 2.b 3.b 4.d 5.a 6.c 7.b

Reading Comprehension:

1. started 2. rejected 3. supported 4. long 5. against

CHAPTER 2

[Unit 1]

Vocab Preview:

A: 1.e 2.a 3.h 4.g 5.b 6.c 7.d 8.f

B: 1. enhance 2. poverty 3. households 4. percentile 5. distribution
6. phenomenon 7. conclude 8. inequality

Language Focus: 1.a 2.a 3.b 4.b 5.d 6.d 7.c

Reading Comprehension:

1. unequal 2. concern 3. enhancing 4. refers 5. poor

[Unit 2]

Vocab Preview:

A: 1.c 2.a 3.h 4.f 5.b 6.g 7.d 8.e

B: 1. stem 2. backbreaking 3. unjustified 4. genre 5. awaken
6. Restrict 7. heritage 8. catastrophe

Language Focus: 1.c 2.b 3.b 4.d 5.b 6.d 7.c

Reading Comprehension:

1. discriminate 2. treated 3. restricting 4. stem 5. awaken

[Unit 3]

Vocab Preview:

A: 1.e 2.f 3.b 4.a 5.h 6.c 7.d 8.g

B: 1. distress 2. interpersonal 3. abusive 4. shelter 5. intentional 6. mitigate 7. dignity 8. neglect

Language Focus: 1.d 2.d 3.a 4.b 5.b 6.c 7.d

Reading Comprehension:

1. defined 2. physically 3. common 4. abusive 5. effects

[Unit 4]

Vocab Preview:

A: 1.d 2.e 3.c 4.g 5.a 6.h 7.f 8.b

B: 1. sustainable 2. omission 3. humane 4. encompass 5. minimize 6. cramped 7. inherently 8. husbandry

Language Focus: 1.d 2.c 3.b 4.b 5.d 6.c 7.d

Reading Comprehension:

1. cruelty 2. encompasses 3. cramped 4. over 5. continuing

[Unit 5]

Vocab Preview:

A: 1.h 2.a 3.e 4.b 5.g 6.c 7.d 8.f

B: 1. imbalance 2. coercion 3. contemporary 4. assert 5. rationalization 6. legal 7. habitual 8. hostile

Language Focus: 1.c 2.a 3.a 4.a 5.b 6.a 7.c

Reading Comprehension:

1. abuse 2. imbalance 3. abuse 4. any 5. divided

[Unit 6]

Vocab Preview:

A: 1.e 2.c 3.g 4.b 5.h 6.d 7.a 8.f

B: 1. exploitation 2. workforce 3. refugee 4. traumatic 5. displaced 6. resettlement 7. buffer 8. integrates

Language Focus: 1.c 2.a 3.d 4.b 5.a 6.b 7.c

Reading Comprehension:

1. displaced 2. consist 3. integrating 4. many 5. often

REFERENCES

General / All Units

Douglas, Nancy & Bohike, David. (2020). Reading Explorer 3. Boston: National Geographic Learning.

Seong, Myeong-Hee& Lewin, Lyle A. (2013). Next Level Toeic. 서울: 지식인.

Seong, Myeong-Hee, Freeman Casey, Lewin, Lyle A. (2013). Total TOEIC. 서울: 지식인.

Seong, Myeong-Hee, Shin, Yoon-Hee& Lewin, Lyle A. (2015). Step One TOEIC. 서울: 지식인.

Seong, Myeong-Hee, Cuffey, Daniel, Choe, Erika &Karcher Chase. (2020). The BigPicture. 서울: 지식인.

CHAPTER 1

[Unit 1]

Topic:

8 Nonverbal Communication Differences Between Cultures. Point Park University Online. (2021, May 25). https://online.pointpark.edu/business/cultural-differences-in-nonverbal-communication/.

Cultural Spotlight:

Lauzen, M. M. (2016). It's a Man's (Celluloid) World. sdsu.edu. https://womenintvfilm.sdsu.edu/files/2015_Its_a_Mans_Celluloid_World_Report.pdf.

Murphy, Jocelyn Nichole, "The role of women in film: Supporting the men — An analysis of how culture influences the changing discourse on gender representations in film" (2015). Journalism Undergraduate Honors Theses. 2. http://scholarworks.uark.edu/jouruht/2

Wikimedia Foundation. (2021, May 26). The Way We Were. Wikipedia. https://en.wikipedia.org/wiki/The_Way_We_Were.

[Unit 2]

Topic:

Samuel Putnam, M. A. G. (2019, January 14). Perspective | How different cultures shape children's personalities in different ways. The Washington Post. https://www.washingtonpost.com/national/health-science/how-different-cultures-shape-childrens-personalities-in-different-ways/2019/01/11/1c059a92-f7de-11e8-8d64-4e79db33382f_story.html.

United Nations. (2019, August 12). International Youth Day. un.org. https://www.un.org/development/desa/youth/wp-content/uploads/sites/21/2019/08/WYP2019_10-Key-Messages_GZ_8AUG19.pdf.

Wikimedia Foundation. (2021, May 27). Youth. Wikipedia. https://en.wikipedia.org/wiki/Youth.

Cultural Spotlight:

Wikimedia Foundation. (2021, May 25). Coming-of-age story. Wikipedia. https://en.wikipedia.org/wiki/Coming-of-age_story.

Wikimedia Foundation. (2021, May 22). Titanic (1997 film). Wikipedia. https://en.wikipedia.org/wiki/Titanic_(1997_film).

[Unit 3]

Topic:

Fielding, S. (2018, April 18). 12 ways wedding traditions differ around the world.

Insider. https://www.insider.com/wedding-traditions-around-the-world-2018-4.

Cultural Spotlight:
Wikimedia Foundation. (2021, May 10). Love Story (1970 film). Wikipedia.
https://en.wikipedia.org/wiki/Love_Story_(1970_film).

[Unit 4]
Topic:
Wikimedia Foundation. (2021, May 27). Supernatural. Wikipedia.
https://en.wikipedia.org/wiki/Supernatural.
Cultural Spotlight:
Wikimedia Foundation. (2021, May 29). Ghost (1990 film). Wikipedia.
https://en.wikipedia.org/wiki/Ghost_(1990_film).

[Unit 5]
Topic:
Guardian News and Media. (2018, August 27). Religion: why faith is becoming more and more popular. The Guardian.
https://www.theguardian.com/news/2018/aug/27/religion-why-is-faith-growing-and-what-happens-next.

Cultural Spotlight:
Wikimedia Foundation. (2021, May 5). Santa Claus. Wikipedia.
https://en.wikipedia.org/wiki/Santa_Claus.

[Unit 6]
Topic:
Wikimedia Foundation. (2021, May 28). Counterculture. Wikipedia.
https://en.wikipedia.org/wiki/Counterculture.

Wikimedia Foundation. (2021, May 30). Hippie. Wikipedia.

https://en.wikipedia.org/wiki/Hippie.

Cultural Spotlight:
Wikimedia Foundation. (2021, May 24). Forrest Gump. Wikipedia. https://en.wikipedia.org/wiki/Forrest_Gump.

CHAPTER 2

[Unit 1]

Topic:
OECD. (2011). An Overview of Growing Income Inequalities in OECD Countries. oecd.org. https://www.oecd.org/els/soc/49499779.pdf.

Wikimedia Foundation. (2021, May 25). Economic inequality. Wikipedia. https://en.wikipedia.org/wiki/Economic_inequality.

Cultural Spotlight:
Wikimedia Foundation. (2021, May 30). Rags to riches. Wikipedia. https://en.wikipedia.org/wiki/Rags_to_riches.

Wikimedia Foundation. (2021, May 23). Robin Hood. Wikipedia. https://en.wikipedia.org/wiki/Robin_Hood.

[Unit 2]

Topic:
Wikimedia Foundation. (2021, May 12). Racism. Wikipedia. https://en.wikipedia.org/wiki/Racism.

Cultural Spotlight:
Amoako, A. (n.d.). Strange Fruit: The most shocking song of all time? BBC Culture.

https://www.bbc.com/culture/article/20190415-strange-fruit-the-most-shocking-song-of-all-time.

[Unit 3]

Topic:
Wikimedia Foundation. (2021, May 28). Child abuse. Wikipedia.
https://en.wikipedia.org/wiki/Child_abuse.

Cultural Spotlight:
Wikimedia Foundation. (2021, May 30). Oprah Winfrey. Wikipedia.
https://en.wikipedia.org/wiki/Oprah_Winfrey.

[Unit 4]

Topic:
Wikimedia Foundation. (2021, May 10). Cruelty to animals. Wikipedia.
https://en.wikipedia.org/wiki/Cruelty_to_animals.

Cultural Spotlight:
Charlotte, Pointing. (2020, December 15). Why Is Veganism on the Rise? LIVEKINDLY. https://www.livekindly.co/why-is-veganism-on-the-rise/.

[Unit 5]

Topic:
Gaines, J. (2019, June 1). Finland is really good at stopping bullying. Here's how they're doing it. Upworthy.
https://www.upworthy.com/finland-is-really-good-at-stopping-bullying-heres-how-theyre-doing-it.

Guardian News and Media. (2013, November 20). How do other countries tackle bullying? The Guardian.

https://www.theguardian.com/teacher-network/teacher-blog/2013/nov/20/other-countries-tackle-bullying.

Cultural Spotlight:
Wikimedia Foundation. (2021, May 2). Dangerous Minds. Wikipedia. https://en.wikipedia.org/wiki/Dangerous_Minds.
Wikimedia Foundation. (2021, April 1). Herd mentality. Wikipedia. https://en.wikipedia.org/wiki/Herd_mentality.

[Unit 6]

Topic:
Dryden-Peterson, Sarah. 2015. The Educational Experiences of Refugee Children in Countries of First Asylum. Washington, DC: Migration Policy Institute. https://www.migrationpolicy.org/sites/default/files/publications/FCD_Dryen-Peterson-FINALWEB.pdf

What is a Refugee? Definition and Meaning: USA for UNHCR. Definition and Meaning | USA for UNHCR. (n.d.). https://www.unrefugees.org/refugee-facts/what-is-a-refugee/.

Cultural Spotlight:
Wikimedia Foundation. (2021, May 22). Imagine (John Lennon song). Wikipedia. https://en.wikipedia.org/wiki/Imagine_(John_Lennon_song).

Unit Pictures

CHAPTER 1

[Unit 1] https://pixabay.com/

[Unit 2] https://pixabay.com/

[Unit 3] https://pixabay.com/

[Unit 4] https://pixabay.com/

[Unit 5] https://pixabay.com/

[Unit 6] https://www.britannica.com/topic/hippie

CHAPTER 2

[Unit 1] https://www.theguardian.com/cities/2017/nov/29/sao-paulo-injustice-tuca-vieira-inequality-photograph-paraisopolis

[Unit 2] https://pixabay.com/

[Unit 3] https://pixabay.com/

[Unit 4] https://pixabay.com/

[Unit 5] https://pixabay.com/

[Unit 6] https://pixabay.com/